SHELBYVILLE
Murders and Mob Justice in a Small Town

By
Terry L. Coats

GRANDPA'S ROAD PUBLISHING
GOODLETTSVILLE, TENNESSEE

© 2025 by Terry L. Coats

All Rights Reserved

No portion of this book may be reproduced in any fashion, either mechanically or electronically, without the express written permission of the author. Short excerpts may be used for media reviews with the author's or publisher's permission.

First Edition, February 2025

Printed in the United States of America on acid-free paper

ISBN 979-8-218-58957-8

Cover design and interior layout by Judy Adamski

Published by and available from:

Grandpa's Road Publishing
226 Swift Drive
Goodlettsville, Tennessee 37072

www.ncstldepots.com

In memory of over 26,000 dedicated men and women in American law enforcement who have lost their lives while bravely serving their communities.

Contents

Author's Note — Page 8

Chapter 1
The Third Murder: NC&St.L Ry. Detective Everson — Page 13
   Saturday, February 10, 1912, 3:36 p.m., Nashville, Tennessee — Page 15
   Plessy v. Ferguson: Separate but Equal — Page 21
   The Two Jim Crow Cars on the No.5 — Page 24
   3:54 p.m., Just Outside Bell Buckle, Tennessee — Page 25

Chapter 2
The Manhunt — Page 35
   Saturday, February 10, 1912, 4:18 p.m. Just Outside Bell Buckle, Tennesse — Page 37

Chapter 3
The First Two Murders: Shelbyville Police Officers
   Redin G. Purdy and Charles Henry — Page 43
   Tuesday, October 31, 1911, 3:15 p.m., Shelbyville, Tennessee — Page 45
   Tuesday, January 2, 1912, 3:00 p.m., Fairfield Tennessee — Page 59
   Friday, January 5, 1912, 4:00 p.m., Davidson County Jail, Nashville, Tennessee — Page 66

Chapter 4
The Marion Anderson Preliminary Hearing
   The Preliminary Hearing — Page 69
   Thursday, February 1, 1912, 9:00 a.m., Shelbyville, Tennessee — Page 71

Chapter 5
A Lynching in Town — Page 85
   Friday, February 16, 1912, 6:00 p.m., Shelbyville, Tennessee — Page 87
   Monday, February 19, 1912, 1:00 p.m., Bedford County Courthouse — Page 89
   2:00 p.m., Bedford County Courthouse — Page 92
   2:05 p.m., Bedford County Courthouse — Page 95
   3:45 p.m., On the Streets of Shelbyville — Page 97

Chapter 6
The First Trial of Marion Anderson — Page 109
    Saturday, April 13, 1912, Shelbyville, Tennessee: Jury Selection — Page 111
    Monday, April 15, 1912, Day One of the Trial — Page 114
    Tuesday, April 16, 1912, Day Two of the Trial — Page 121
    Wednesday, April 17, 1912, Day Three of the Trial — Page 134

Chapter 7
The Second Trial of Marion Anderson — Page 145
    Monday, July 1, 1912, Shelbyville, Tennessee — Page 147

Chapter 8
Aftermath — Page 153

Chapter 9
A History of Lynching in America — Page 159
    Lynching in Colonial America — Page 161
    Slave Codes — Page 164
    Lynching and Vigilantism in the Pre-Civil War Years — Page 168
    The Years of War and Reconstruction (1861-1877) — Page 169
    Lynching 1877 to 1955 — Page 175
        The Red Scare — Page 183
        The Omaha Courthouse Lynching of 1919 — Page 187
        World War II, 1941-1945 — Page 189
        Civil Rights Advancements in the 1950s and 1960s — Page 196
        Congress Passes Anti-Lynching Law, 2022 — Page 200

Acknowledgments and Credits — Page 203

References — Page 204

Author's Note

This is my second book. My first publication, *Next Stop on Grandpa's Road—History and Architecture of NC&St.L Railway Depots and Terminals*, was published in 2010. That was a reference book on the history of the Nashville, Chattanooga and St. Louis Railway from 1845 to 1957 and featured over 600 photographs of NC&St.L stations, terminals, and other railroad structures. In this book, *Shelbyville*, I have chosen to depart from the reference style I used in my first book. My goal is to recount the murder of three law enforcement officers and the difficulties encountered by the county sheriff in preventing the lynching of the suspected killers. In one instance, he was successful; in another, he experienced a dismal failure.

I served as a police officer with the Metropolitan Nashville Police Department for 30 years. Additionally, I am currently the president of the Nashville, Chattanooga and St. Louis Preservation Society, a historical organization dedicated to preserving NC&St.L railroad history.

Several years ago, my experiences in law enforcement, combined with my passion for railroad history, led me to uncover the story of the 1912 murder of NC&St.L Railway Detective Squire W. Everson, as well as the murders of two city policemen in Shelbyville, Tennessee.

Between Halloween night 1911 and the second week of February 1912, quiet Bedford County, Tennessee, which had not experienced a serious crime in decades, was suddenly faced with the brutal murders of three law enforcement officers within its jurisdiction.

While visiting the Officer Down Memorial, a website honoring over 26,000 American police officers who have lost their lives in the line of duty since America's founding in 1776, I read about the loss of my fellow officers from the Nashville Police Department. This prompted me to expand my search to see if any NC&St.L railroad officers had also fallen in the line of duty. During my research, I discovered the record of Detective Felix G. Presson, an NC&St.L policeman who was killed in 1937 during a shootout with a vagabond in Memphis, Tennessee. As I continued reading about this incident, further research led me to the murder case from 1912 involving NC&St.L Detective Everson, a case I had not previously known about.

This book is a work of creative nonfiction—a genre of writing that combines literary styles and techniques to create factually accurate narratives. It covers three murders, the police work to discover the identity of suspects, two preliminary hearings, and the two criminal trials that followed.

Unfortunately, I could not obtain the original transcripts of these court proceedings, so I am unable to quote them directly. It is likely that no transcripts exist for the preliminary hearings, as they were primarily held to determine whether there was enough evidence to proceed to a full trial; transcripts of these hearings were usually not recorded. Despite extensive efforts, I was also unable to locate a transcript of the two trials involving Marion Anderson, the man charged with the murders of the two city policemen. By the time I began my research, more than a hundred years had passed since these events, and I suspect that the original transcripts were destroyed when a lynch mob burned down the Bedford County Courthouse in December 1934. In some instances, I created minimal dialogue to clarify points of interest or to advance the story. I assigned fictitious names to a few characters related to the train portion of the narrative, such as dispatchers and station agents; these men had no direct connection to the murders or the actual participants.

In the absence of firsthand transcripts, I relied on secondary sources, particularly newspaper coverage of the trials. Fortunately, since Shelbyville is situated approximately halfway between Nashville and

Chattanooga, both the *Nashville Tennessean* and the *Chattanooga Times* took a significant interest in the murders of the two Shelbyville policemen and the lynching of the two Black men charged with the murder of the railroad detective. Both newspapers provided extensive coverage, allowing me to develop a detailed overview of the events surrounding Marion Anderson's murders of two of Shelbyville's finest and the subsequent trials.

To capture the local perspective, I turned to the hometown *Shelbyville Gazette* to see how they reported the events. However, much to my disappointment, I found that all copies of the Gazette from 1911 to 1914 were missing from both the Tennessee State Library and Archives, as well as from the local Bedford County Historical Society Library.

All discussions concerning the capture of the three suspects involved in the murder of the railroad detective, as well as the sole suspect in the murders of the two city officers and the trial of that suspect, are reported verbatim whenever possible, based on newspaper sources. I chose not to correct any grammatical errors or alter the dialogue.

As with most trials, there were contradictions in witness testimonies in the Anderson case. I did not attempt to determine which witness was telling the truth or which version was accurate. Whenever I encountered discrepancies in testimony, I included a note in parentheses to clarify.

This book is divided into three parts.

The first part explores the murder of S.W. Everson, a detective for the NC&St.L Railway, along with the arrest and subsequent lynching of two suspects in that case.

The second part focuses on the murders of Shelbyville officers Redin Purdy and Charles Henry, detailing the suspect's escape, capture, and trials.

The third part, which is the final chapter, provides an in-depth examination of the tragic and gruesome history of lynching in America.

When the No.5 left Nashville, little did anyone know the events of February 10, 1912, would take an ugly turn. Three NC&St.L Railway employees, brothers Wat Greer and David Neal, and a third man, Charles Dane Bomar, would be charged with the murder of S.W. Everson, a railroad detective, and within two weeks, two of these three men would be dead at the hands of a lynch mob.

Mob: | mäb | noun a large crowd of people, especially one that is disorderly and intent on causing trouble or violence: a mob of protesters.
—*New Oxford American Dictionary*

Chapter One

The Third Murder:
NC&St.L Ry. Detective Everson
"Let's throw this son-of-a-bitch off the train."

Saturday, February 10, 1912, 3:36 p.m., Nashville, Tennessee

In early December 1911, Niagara Falls froze solid. In the northeast United States, that month, and for months to come, temperature records were broken, some of which had stood for almost 60 years. Likewise, the southern region of the United States had not been immune from the same winter blast. On this cold, drizzly day, Nashville Chattanooga & St. Louis Railway (NC&St.L Ry.) No.5, the daily train between Nashville, Tennessee, and Atlanta, Georgia, was waiting for departure from Nashville's Union Station. The train was sitting on track number 3, nestled under the massive 500-foot-long train shed on the south side of the terminal. No.5 would soon depart on its 450-mile trek to the Peach Tree City of Atlanta.

A light dusting of snow deposited the night before swirled around the Union Station platforms, and just outside the station, the trees glistened with the shimmering ice crystals of pogonip.

NC&St.L Conductor W.L. Sampson, sitting in the operator's office on the basement floor of Union Station, looked up to see Robert Kincaid enter the office. Kincaid would be the engineer on No.5. Sampson and Kincaid, seasoned veterans of the railroad, had worked this run to Atlanta together for many years. Upon entering, the engineer obtained a duplicate copy of the orders Conductor Sampson had been perusing from the operator. Walking from the office toward their waiting train, Kincaid read aloud the orders as Sampson followed along from his copy.

By synchronizing the reading of the orders, neither man would have a question about how the train's operation would be conducted or at what location No.5 would encounter an opposing train. The orders would control No.5's movements and the meeting points with other trains during the Nashville-to-Chattanooga leg of their run.

The orders signified that No.5 would have the right of way over the three freight trains they would meet at Christiana, Sherwood, and Cowan, Tennessee. But they would also meet train No.94, The Dixie Flyer, a crack Chicago-to-Florida NC&St.L express train at Normandy, Tennessee. Since No.5 was designated as a local passenger train, No.94 would be the superior train for the scheduled meeting. No.5 would be required to take the siding at Normandy to allow the Express to pass unimpeded.

No.5 would leave a few minutes past its scheduled 3:30 p.m. departure time. The Union Station stationmaster held No.5, awaiting the late arrival of the Nashville & Louisville Railroad's Louisville Accommodation, due at 2:55 p.m. Unlike an Express train that would make few, if any, stops between major cities, an Accommodation train would make stops at most if not all of the smaller ones.

Several passengers from the L&N train needed to make the connection for Chattanooga. The southbound would hold, awaiting the arrival of the accommodation train. Within a couple of minutes of the arrival of the late-running Louisville train, the passengers from that train who wanted to transfer to the No.5 hurriedly made their way across the icy platform and made the reassignment. A young mother, baby in arms and holding fast to the hand of her 5-year-old son, was the last to cross the platform between the trains to the waiting coach car of No.5.

With the two trains sitting on adjacent tracks, a transfer was made between the Rail Post Office (RPO) and the baggage cars of the inbound L&N train to the sister cars on No.5. To the RPO car went several parcels and a large canvas bag of mail destined for post offices southeast of Nashville. The passengers' luggage traveling toward Atlanta was transferred to the baggage car.

With the transfers made, the giant freight door on No.5's RPO slammed shut with a resounding BANG! With the luggage and parcels loaded and all the passengers aboard, it was time to depart.

Conductor Sampson tugged on the long gold chain leading to his pocket and retrieved the Hamilton pocket watch he kept there. The watch's hands displayed the time as 3:36. Just after noting the time, he recorded it in a small pocket-sized log book he kept in the vest of his uniform coat. When time allowed, he duplicated that information in a "Passenger Conductor's Report to Superintendent Form," as required by the railroad.

Engineer Robert Kincaid watched intently for the conductor's signal to proceed. With the late arrival of the L&N, the minutes lost would have to be made up to keep to the railroad's published timetable schedule and to make the meets of the other trains as stipulated in the orders he and the conductor had received before boarding their train.

In the fading light of this February afternoon, Conductor Sampson, still standing on the station platform, called, "All aboard." As he looked toward the locomotive, he did a final check of the cars in the consist. Stepping into the vestibule of the trailing Pullman car, he raised and lowered the kerosene lantern in his right hand in a quick up-and-down motion. The lantern's dim glow was barely visible to Kincaid, but it was the signal he had been waiting for. The signal meant that all was well through to the end of the train, and it granted permission to the engineer to ease the train away from the station.

Kincaid reached over his head and grabbed the wooden handle

attached at the locomotive's roof by a cotton cord. With three pulls on the handle, a valve opened, allowing a blast of 500-degree steam to race through the pipe. This resulted in a deep baritone tone that belched from the brass three-chime whistle mounted on top of the locomotive's boiler.

The blasts of the whistle resounded off the rafters of the massive train shed behind Union Station. Echoing upward, the sound deflected one more time off the dagger-sharp, silver-blue icicles dangling on the eves of the roof.

The whistle was the notice to No.5's conductor and the train crew that the engineer was about to notch out the throttle of locomotive #345, a 2-8-0 Consolidation class of the NC&St.L fleet. The locomotive and its ward of ten passenger cars were about to creep slowly from the terminal, headed to Georgia.

A steam locomotive operates on a combination of fire and water. On the opposite side of the locomotive's cab, 24-year-old fireman Jeff Conner glanced at the steam pressure gauge mounted just below his eye level on the face of the firebox. The 200-psi shown on the gauge was the amount of pressure needed to start the iron behemoth moving. It would be of the utmost importance that he maintain the proper steam pressure to keep the locomotive operating at its most efficient level, and most critically, he needed to ensure sufficient water was flowing into the locomotive's boiler. Failure to maintain the proper amount of water would allow the locomotive to overheat, resulting in catastrophic explosive consequences. Besides seeing sufficient water flowing to the boiler, Conner's responsibility until they reached Chattanooga would be to resume feeding bituminous coal to the hungry mouth of the locomotive firebox. The fireman, a vast shovel full of coal in hand, stepped on a foot pedal controlling the two iron doors on the mouth of the firebox. Pressure on the pedal forced the doors to rise in opposing directions, something akin to the wings of an angel unfolding. The fireman exposed himself to an enormous blast of blistering heat each time the doors opened. Conner wore green-tinted safety glasses, and a bandanna pulled up to cover his mouth and nose. The tinted glasses protected his eyes from the glow of the fire, and the bandanna gave him a modicum of protection from the searing heat—and from inhaling the tiny burning embers and the unburned coal dust.

A big part of his job as a fireman was surveying the glowing coals on the firebox floor and quickly determining where to distribute each shovel of coal he would feed to the firebox. After spreading a shovel of coal to its appropriate place, he would return to the tender behind the locomotive and retrieve another shovel full of coal from the bunker. Time after time, shovel after shovel, the process started anew.

Puffs of blue-black smoke and whiffs of expended steam from the cylinders combined and belched into the frosty air from the red-colored-capped stack atop the locomotive. Anyone in Nashville familiar with the local railroads would quickly identify that capped stack and the bright red paint as standard on every NC&St.L system locomotive. As each exhaust cycle was dispatched into the cold, crisp air and the giant drive wheels of the locomotive made a one-quarter revolution, a familiar ...chuff ...chuff ...chuff ...chuff sounded as the locomotive and cars slowly began to move from the platform.

The cars of No.5 were filled almost to capacity this Saturday afternoon.

Weekend days were a busy time for the NC&St.L. Consistently, passengers traveling at week's end filled the trains almost to capacity. Businessmen and drummers who had been away from their families were traveling back to home base. They were glad to be getting back to their families. Young couples who had moved to the larger cities away from their rural roots were returning to see old friends. Ladies who wanted to do a little shopping "in the city" took the opportunity to travel on the weekends.

The train's consist directly behind locomotive #345 and her tender included, in this order, a Rail Post Office car, a baggage car, and three segregated "Jim Crow" cars for the Black patrons. Three coaches and two Pullman sleeping cars brought up the train's rear.

The Jim Crow cars were a sign of the times. They came into existence through several landmark decisions by the United States Supreme Court and several political maneuvers over the years since the Civil War.

The Compromise of 1876, an informal agreement between the Democrat party and affiliates of presidential candidate Rutherford B. Hayes, a Republican, effectively ended the Reconstruction era in the South. The agreement allowed Hayes to ascend to the presidency over his opponent, Democrat candidate Governor Samuel B. Tilden of New York. In return, the Republicans would withdraw Federal troops from all Southern states. Additionally, Southern Democrats promised to protect the civil and political rights of Blacks. As it turned out, these promises were not kept. Widespread disenfranchisement of Black voters was ramped up. With the end of federal interference, southern legislatures began passing legislation known as "Jim Crow Laws." (Jim Crow was a character in a popular 1800s minstrel show song.) These laws required the separation of Whites from "persons of color" in restaurants and theaters, on public transportation, including railroads, and in any other location where the two races might intermingle.

In 1881, Tennessee passed a law (1881 TN Public Chapter CLV) as an addendum to an 1875 Act.

The new law mandated:
    [R]ailroad companies must provide separate cars for colored passengers

who paid first-class rates. These cars were to be kept in good repair and subject to the same rules as other first-class cars, to prevent smoking and obscene language.

A progenitor act, Chapter 130 of the Acts of Tennessee in 1875, had set precedence for the "Crow" laws by allowing for discrimination in public places. No longer was discrimination limited to trains and streetcars but now extended to hotels, restaurants, theaters, circuses, museums, and steamboats.

The Tennessee law was a forerunner of the separate but equal decision in *Plessy v. Ferguson*.

Plessy v. Ferguson: **Separate but Equal**

An 1887 Florida law mandated railroads operating within that state to furnish segregated accommodations for both Black and White races. Before the end of the century, similar laws were adopted by states across the South. The states demanded that the railroads operating within their jurisdiction enforce this law. In 1890, the Louisiana State Legislature passed the "Separate Car Act," similar to the Florida law requiring separate accommodations. Under Louisiana law, a train conductor was required to assign seating according to race.

This law was unpopular with the railroads. It added expenses and labor for the companies to implement the requirements. It was obviously also unpopular with Blacks, who saw it as another erosion of rights granted to them under the 13th and 14th Amendments of the U.S. Constitution.

On June 7, 1892, New Orleans shoemaker Homère Patrice Adolphe Plessy (Homer), an "octoroon" (a person of seven-eighths White and one-eighth Black ancestry), bought a first-class ticket and boarded a "Whites Only" car of the East Louisiana Railroad in New Orleans.

Plessy was told he could not sit there after taking his seat in the train's first-class "Whites Only" car. The conductor insisted he vacate his seat and remove himself to one of the seats in the Blacks-only segregated car of the train. Plessy had been born a free man and was so fair-skinned that he easily passed as a White man. However, under Louisiana law, he was classified as Black and thus required to sit in one of the "colored" cars. He refused.

This incident with Plessy was a pre-arranged and orchestrated event by the East Louisiana Railroad and a group called the Comité des Citoyens. The railroad company opposed the Separate Car Act on financial grounds. Fulfilling the requirements of the law would require the purchase of railcars for its White patrons and additional ones for the Black patrons. The Comité des Citoyens (Committee of Citizens in French), a group of prominent Black Creoles and White Creole New Orleans residents, formed a civil rights group dedicated to repealing the Separate Car Act and fighting its implementation. The Comité persuaded Plessy to participate in this staged event to challenge the Act.

The railroad company had been informed in advance of the Comité's plan to challenge the Act. To prepare for the challenge, the Comité hired a private detective with arrest powers to detain Plessy. The detective aimed to avoid charging Plessy with a lesser offense, such as vagrancy, and instead focused on the specific Act they wanted to challenge.

Plessy was arrested and remanded for trial in Orleans Parish. The trial was intended to test the merits of what would become known as the separate but equal clause in a Louisiana State Court.

In court, the Prosecution cited the 1890 Louisiana law stating that separate but equal was legal. Plessy, through his attorneys, argued the law was unconstitutional. The trial judge, J.H. Ferguson, sided with the government after hearing the evidence. The case was appealed to the Louisiana Supreme Court when Plessy's attorney filed a Writ of Prosecution to keep Ferguson from enforcing the law. The Louisiana Supreme Court ruled against Plessy, upholding the statute as constitutional.

In 1896, the case went to the United States Supreme Court. In the case of *Plessy v. Ferguson*, the High Court ruled that racial segregation laws, many of which had been in effect since the days of Reconstruction, did not violate the United States Constitution as long as the facilities for each race were equal in quality.

In this historic case, Associate Supreme Court Justice Henry Billings Brown, writing for the majority, stated that the 14th Amendment to the Constitution was intended to ensure equality under the law but not to eliminate racial distinctions. He argued, "Political equality of the races is not compromised by segregation." The decision ruled that state laws establishing racially segregated facilities did not violate the equal protection clause if those facilities were deemed "separate but equal."

In a dissenting vote, Associate Justice John Marshall Harlan argued that the Louisiana law was discriminatory as it segregated Black passengers from coaches designated for White passengers. He contended that the law aimed to prevent Black individuals from associating with Whites, constituting a violation of civil rights.

With the Court's ruling, the "separate-but-equal" doctrine opened all manner of doors for states to continue enforcing Jim Crow laws regulating the separation by race in public facilities and accommodations. On the railroads, this meant "Jim Crow" cars.

It would take 58 years for the 1896 *Plessy v. Ferguson* decision to be overturned. On May 17, 1954, the Supreme Court issued a unanimous ruling that significantly impacted America. The Court found that state-sanctioned segregation of public schools violated the 14th Amendment. This ruling, known as *Brown v. Board of Education of Topeka,* overturned *Plessy* and held that "separate-but-equal" education and other services were not, in fact, equal at all. This principle of separate but equal was the catapult that launched the Jim Crow era.

The Two Jim Crow Cars on the No.5

In 1912, America was a segregated country. *The Brown v. Board of Education of Topeka* ruling was a mere dream. Citing the "separate but equal" clause, all United States railroads established apartheid, mandating that Blacks ride in cars explicitly designated for their race. Thus, on the No.5 train that day, every Black person on the train, save two Negro porters who were working their assigned positions, would be traveling in one of these segregated "Crow cars."

Crow cars, like most cars of the era, were of wooden construction. Even in years to come, when the NC&St.L and other railroads could afford to upgrade their passenger cars to newer all-steel construction, few, if any, of these cars were replaced.[1]

---

[1] The railroad purchased some of the Jim Crow cars in the 1880s, and they were still in revenue service after the 1957 merger of the NC&St.L Railway and the Louisville & Nashville R.R. In 1961, one of the old L&N cars was pulled from retirement and returned to service; it was painted bright yellow and would accompany the famous Western and Atlantic Railroad engine "The General" for the 100th-anniversary tour celebrating the centennial of the War Between the States.

On the morning of July 9, 1918, two passenger trains on the NC&St.L collided head-on five miles west of Nashville. Each of the trains contained Jim Crow cars. The wooden construction of these cars played a deadly role in this tragic accident. Most of the 100-plus fatalities occurred in two of the Crow cars. An investigation conducted by the Interstate Commerce Commission revealed that the number of deaths could have been reduced if the cars had been constructed of steel instead of wood. To this day, the Dutchman's Curve accident remains the deadliest passenger train accident in the history of the United States.

3:54 p.m., Just Outside Bell Buckle, Tennessee

All NC&St.L employees held employee passes for free transportation on most NC trains for themselves and their families. It was common practice for an employee to use the complimentary transportation by catching a Nashville-bound train to carry them to the capital city where their workweek started. Likewise, the reverse would take place at the end of the week, when they would board an outbound train headed back home.

In the second of these segregated cars on the train were several Black railway employees. Among them were Charles (Wat) Greer and his half-brother Dave Neal. Both men were residents of Shelbyville, Tennessee, a town about 50 miles southeast of Nashville. Both worked for the NC&St.L as track construction crew members known as section hands or "gandy dancers." ("Gandy dancers" was probably coined to describe the "dancing" movements of the men working as they pushed against the long steel toolbars they used to nudge the rails into position. The dancing would often be timed along with a chant, keeping their movements in unison.)

It had been a long, hard week for the brothers, brought on by the freezing, snowy weather that had beset the Middle Tennessee area. The cold weather had been incredibly destructive to the steel rails and the roadbed, which these construction crews were responsible for repairing.

Greer and Neal were delighted to be returning home to their families. They eagerly anticipated home-cooked meals and the warmth of their homes, sheltered from the harsh winter that had taken a toll on them physically. The NC&St.L did not run a train directly to Shelbyville. The half-brothers would need to disembark from the No.5 at a scheduled stop in Wartrace, Tennessee, and then board an accommodation train designated to meet the arrival of the No.5 each day. The accommodation train was a short train consisting of a locomotive, a tender, and two or three passenger cars. After the passengers transferred from the mainline train, the accommodation train would travel eight miles to the end of the branch in Shelbyville.

Having an accommodation train assigned to the branch would allow passengers to go to Shelbyville without diverting a mainline train, which has been the norm since the railroad arrived in the county.

In 1845, Vernon K. Stevenson, the first president of the Nashville and Chattanooga Railroad (N&C), and John E. Thomson, the railroad's head Civil Engineer, traveled on horseback to survey the land and plot the location of what would eventually become the right-of-way between the two named cities.[2] Thomson's survey proposed taking the railroad not through Shelbyville but instead through the northeast side of Bedford County, of which Shelbyville was the county seat.

In 1847, the N&C Railroad began construction in Nashville, southeastward toward Chattanooga. By the summer of the following year, the railroad had reached the outskirts of Bedford County. If the county commissioners had their way, the railroad would have bypassed the county entirely. The county commissioners shared the opinions of many communities of that time. They wanted no part of what they perceived to be noisy, dirty, smoke-belching locomotives or the supposed disruption, harmful elements, and the riffraff the railroad would surely bring.

On the other hand, the city fathers in Shelbyville were disheartened to find the inter-city mainline had passed them by. They saw the railroad as an opportunity to bring commerce and prosperity to the city.

In many cases, entire towns closed and moved to a new location to settle the community along the rails. It was essential to have the services and transportation the railroads could provide. The town of Shelbyville did not relocate. Instead, they did the next best thing. As soon as the Nashville and Chattanooga Railroad completed construction through the county, the city of Shelbyville allocated money for construction and had the railroad build a branch line eight miles north to the connecting town of Wartrace, Tennessee.

Since mid-summer, the NC&St.L had started assigning one of its railroad detectives to ride aboard designated trains along its system. These detectives were, in their day, similar to the sky marshals assigned to air travel five decades later.

In February 1912, Special Agent Squire Willard (S.W.) Everson had only worked as a detective for the NC&St.L for just over a year. Before joining the NC&St.L, he worked as a carpenter in Nashville. Additionally, he had held a second job as a deputy fire marshal under Davidson County Sheriff Samuel H. Borman in Nashville. His time with the sheriff's office had increased his interest in law enforcement. His job as a railroad detective with the N&C offered him a higher salary than his carpenter job. The increase in his take-home pay would help cover the household expenses of his wife and their three daughters.

On this Saturday, Everson had been assigned to be the onboard security on train No.5. Tensions were running high. Two weeks before, the 57-year-old special agent and one of the two half-brothers, Wat Greer, had had heated words. Greer had gotten so angry he had threatened to cut off the officer's head and throw it out a window. Everson intervened when Greer and a man on another train almost went to fisticuffs. A shouting match erupted between the two men. If the detective had not interposed, the situation would have escalated out of control.

Wat Greer was a heavy drinker. When he stepped up from the platform in Nashville to enter the segregated Crow car at the front of the train, he was already heavily intoxicated. Witnesses later reported that he, Dave Neal, and an acquaintance, Dane Bomar, started passing around a quart bottle of Old Grand-Dad whiskey before they had taken their seats in the car.

As the journey of train No.5 continued, the three passengers consumed more liquor. When the quart bottle they had been sharing ran out, Greer was not content to sit quietly or to sleep until they reached the stop at Wartrace. Instead, he began searching through the three Jim Crow cars for anyone who might have more whiskey.

Aboard the train, Greer found 19-year-old Sam Brooks. The young man was well known to all of the workmen aboard. Sam was a regular part of the track maintenance crew on which Greer and Neal worked. The NC&St.L employees referred to Sam as a "gopher" as he, while working, would "go for this" and "go for that" when someone on the work crews needed something from a toolshed or if they had some other need. Among Sam's responsibilities was carrying a water bucket and a dipper to supply the men working on the track crews with a refreshing drink.

As Brooks was generally known to carry other wet goods (liquor) in addition to his water supply when these men were working, Greer felt sure the boy would be holding a clandestine bottle on the train that night. Greer's speculation turned out to be correct.

Greer first asked Brooks for a draw on the bottle the boy had stashed in his trouser pocket, but when Brooks refused, the drunkard attempted to take the pint of whiskey by force. The young man fought back. Greer was still carrying the empty quart bottle from which he had just finished drinking the content. In his anger at the boy's refusal to share the bottle he was carrying, he raised it to shoulder height and brought it down against the young man's forehead. Stunned, Brooks lost his grip on the bottle, which was now in his hand. The bottle fell to the floor, spilling some of the golden-brown liquid. Greer reached down and rescued the bottle before it gave up the entirety of its contents.

A news butcher, a young boy responsible for selling newspapers, candy, cigars, and other items to passengers, witnessed a commotion and hurried back one car to inform Detective Everson about the disturbance. Upon entering the Jim Crow car, Everson observed the commotion and proceeded to investigate the cause.

The detective questioned Brooks about what had caused the disruption. It seemed to the officer that though the assailant had struck the young man in the head, he was not seriously injured. The officer was trying not to escalate the situation. Everson ordered the two men to quell the argument and then told Greer to return the bottle to its owner. Greer returned the pint bottle to the boy at the officer's insistence, but he would not be appeased.

To Everson, the matter was over; to Wat Greer, the case was far from finished. Agent Everson looked over his shoulder at the two men, thinking the issue had been resolved. When Greer returned the liquor, Everson started to return to the car from which he had been summoned.

Greer returned to his seat, but filled with resentment for having been castigated, he rose and began following the agent toward the middle of the car. Now, only a few inches from Everson, Greer reached out and pushed the detective in his back. He intended to hurry the officer out of the car. Adding to the physical attack, he threatened the officer by telling him to leave the car and that if he were to return, he "would kill him."

Greer had every intent of making good on his threat.

As Everson reached the end of the car, an agitated Greer intensified his harassment. When Neal saw that his brother had reignited the argument, he jumped from his seat and yelled, "Let's throw this son-of-a-bitch off the train."

Greer grabbed the officer by his arm, twirling him halfway around. As Everson completed the turn, he saw that he was facing Greer and also Greer's half-brother. For a brief moment, the detective saw a reflection of light bouncing off the blade of what appeared to be a knife or maybe a straight razor. There was fury in the eyes of both assailants; there was no question about their intent.

The animosity that had started two weeks before when the detective and Greer had had cross words was now exploding into total hostility.

Both brothers laid hands on the detective, one man in front and the other somewhat to the side.

We sometimes find ourselves involved in situations that are not of our own making. Such was the case with Charles Bomar, the co-worker of the two brothers, who now engaged in what would become a deadly struggle between the two men and the detective. Suddenly, Bomar found himself in the fray occurring directly beside his seat. In what would be a life-changing occurrence for him, he sided with the brothers against the detective. Bomar sprang to his feet and advanced toward the skirmish.

Everson was convinced he was about to be overpowered by the

three men. Struggling, he was able to draw his service weapon from its holster. In an attempt to use the weapon as a club, the officer was able to raise the weapon just high enough to bring the barrel of the pistol downward with great force against the head of one of his assailants. The blow landed just to the side of Wat Greer's left eye—opening a large gash. A stream of blood burst forth from the wound, splattering Everson across the face.

Enraged by the struggle, the men latched onto Everson with even more vigor. With one dragging and the other two pushing, Neal, Greer, and Bomar wrestled the now overpowered Everson up the aisle of the passenger car. They forced him through the car's end door and onto the open-air vestibule.

Squire Everson stood just under six feet tall. Because of the demanding physicality he had expended in his employment as a carpenter, he had developed a very muscular physique; still, he was no match for three men bent on overpowering him.

Now, in fear for his life, and with the assailants trying to wrestle his weapon away, Everson attempted again to bring the pistol up in self-defense, but the odds were against him. He was unable to point the pistol directly at any of the men, but he was able to slip his finger past the trigger guard of the weapon and squeeze off a shot.

A yellow-red flash blasted from the muzzle, and the smell of cordite filled the nostrils of all four men. The bullet dispatched from the service revolver, a Smith & Wesson .38, passed through the canvas overcoat of the older brother, slightly grazing him in his lower back. So close together had the three assailants been that the discharge from the pistol set Greer's coat ablaze. Before it could be extinguished, a hole the size of a man's fist had been burned through the cloth.

The small town of Bell Buckle is located 40 miles southeast of

Nashville. For the last two-and-one-half miles of the approach into the city, No.5 was on a downgrade and traveling at around 55 mph.

In response to the small cast metal sign at the trackside, engineer Kincaid gave a long single blast on the locomotive whistle one mile from the station. The "station one mile" sign is oval-shaped and displays a single (-) horizontal bar. The long blast on the whistle would signal to the station agent that the train would arrive momentarily, giving the agent a few moments to alert passengers to prepare for boarding and organize any parcels that might need to be dispatched to the train.

As the station came into the view of the engineer, he notched back the throttle on his locomotive and prepared to bring his train to a gentle stop. As he approached the town, little did he know that behind his locomotive, a life-and-death struggle was playing out in the vestibule of one of the train's passenger cars. An argument over a bottle of liquor had turned into a deadly endeavor.

At this point, the brothers were truly enraged. In what could have been compared to an attack of three lions on a wildebeest, the detective was fighting with all his might to dispel the violence being pressed upon him by dislodging the straight razor from Wat Greer's hand.

Dave Neal grabbed the pistol with both hands, wrenching it out of the right hand of the officer and knocking it to the platform floor beside their feet. With the weapon dispatched, Neal, Greer, and Bomar were free to overwhelm the individual before them. After just a moment of struggle, Everson was at the mercy of the three men. The detective could see the countryside passing at almost 55 miles per hour through the vestibule's open window.

Suddenly, the men had him off his feet and forced him toward the car vestibule's trap door. Still fighting for his life, Everson made a futile grasp for the side of the car window. His efforts were all in vain. Detective S.W. Everson hung suspended mid-air momentarily, but a moment later, gravity prevailed.

Special Agent Everson died instantly upon striking the rough gravel ballast along the tracks. A medical examiner would later determine that Everson's cause of death had been a broken neck caused by hitting the ground after being thrown from the moving train.

In railroad parlance, the station at Bell Buckle was known as a "whistle-stop," meaning that the regularly scheduled train would make a stop there only if someone on the train needed to detrain at that location or if someone at that station requested the train to stop so they might board.

On this cold and blustery Saturday evening, train No.5 would have to make a stop at the station. A few NC&St.L employees who were making their way home from Nashville had requested a stop. The train came to a squealing halt, and three passengers alighted onto the station platform.

As the whistle sounded three short blasts indicating that once again No.5 was about to move forward, there were now five fewer people on the passenger manifest. Gone were the three passengers for the Bell Buckle stop, the railroad detective, and Wat Greer. As the train slowed to make the station stop, Greer swung off the side of the last of the three "Crow" cars on the train and dropped off onto the ballast below, his heavy work boots making a resounding crunch, crunch, crunch in the gravel as he ran away. Knowing that he was in deep trouble and that it could be mere minutes before he would be the subject of a search party for the killing of a White man, Greer made his way back up the tracks toward Nashville to a railroad section house.[3] After stopping at the section house for a few minutes, he started on a circuitous route to perceived safety away from the tracks.

---

[3] A section house was a NC&St.L-owned structure used to house the families of two railroad workers who worked as repair and maintenance men on the tracks. The men's job was to keep a particular "section" of the track in first class condition. Because Greer was a resident of Bedford County as well as an employee of the NC&St.L, it stands to reason that he was aware of the house and even the residents therein.

Chapter Two

The Manhunt

Saturday, February 10, 1912, 4:18 p.m.
Just Outside Bell Buckle, Tennessee

Just one-tenth of a mile north of the depot, the broken, crumpled body of NC&St.L Detective Squire W. Everson lay beside the tracks. His remains had been found just minutes after the train's passing by a local townsman, James Brown, who was making his way into Bell Buckle to buy supplies. Mr. Brown would later say that when he found Everson's body, he first thought the man to be asleep. "He lay on the ground, arms extended as though attempting to make a snow angel on the snowless earth." But it soon became apparent that the situation was much more dire. On closer examination, it was evident that the head and neck of the man were cocked at a very peculiar angle to his body and that he was dead.

Running ahead to the depot, Brown sounded the alarm to A.J. Waters, the station master. Waters, Brown, and two other men who had been in the depot ran back along the tracks to find the lifeless remains of Detective Everson. It immediately became evident from the cuts, abrasions, and bloody, disheveled clothing that the man had either jumped or had been thrown from a passing train.

"Oh my God, it's Detective Everson!" exclaimed Waters. After hitting the ballast and crossties of the track and then tumbling for a short distance, the detective's body had sustained numerous breaks, tears, and abrasions. Even in that condition, Mr. Waters immediately recognized the detective. The two had met a few months back when Everson had worked a case of theft of railroad property in Bell Buckle.

By 7:30 p.m., a group of men in Wartrace had found Wat Greer and captured him by armed force. He emerged near the railroad tracks, muddy and wet from his attempt to cross the creek back and forth.

After he was discovered, Greer did not volunteer to come along peacefully. The men who had surrounded him at the time of his capture took liberty in making him pay for his reluctance to peacefully surrender. When presented at Sheriff James "Big Jim" Williams's office in Shelbyville a short while later, Greer was suffering from a bloody lip, a colossal pump knot on the side of his head, and several bruises and abrasions. Had some of Sheriff Williams' men not been present at the time of the capture, Greer might well have never been brought alive to the sheriff's office; he might have been lynched at the instant of his capture.

Dave Neal stayed on the train, avoiding capture before it slowed to arrive in Wartrace. Like Greer had done outside of Bell Buckle, when the train slowed to a manageable speed for stopping at the station, Neal jumped off the still-moving train and entered the darkness away from the tracks. He knew he would be captured immediately if he got off at the station and tried to catch the No.227 branch line train to Shelbyville.

Within a few hours, Neal had walked the eight miles from Wartrace to Shelbyville. There, he sought asylum in a community just outside of town named Dogtown. Dogtown was the nickname given to the Black community a short distance from the tracks and just north of town.

Upon reaching a familiar dilapidated shack, long in years but still maintained, Neal rapped on the door. A man in his late 70s, walking with the help of a cane, answered the knocking. There was a very brief but desperate conversation, and a moment later, Neal was inside, the door locked tightly behind him.

Dave Neal's clandestine entrance into Dogtown had not escaped the observant eyes of several residents. When Sheriff Williams and some of his deputies descended on the community, it was not long before the residents pointed to the dwelling at the end of the street as the hiding place of the subject of the sheriff's search.

When confronted by the authorities, Neal surrendered without resistance. Sheriff Williams was somewhat taken aback by the fact that he had given up with such ease. Neal was well known to Bedford County law enforcement and was known by all to have the reputation as a real "badass." In fact, throughout previous encounters with law enforcement personnel, he certainly had not given up easily. Dave Neal was about as grisly as an old junkyard dog. He was no stranger to confrontation. During one previous arrest, he had had his left eye shot out; in another, the middle finger of his left hand had been shot off; and in a third arrest, he had been wounded by a bullet to the foot.

By midnight, both men were in custody and, after being carried back to Shelbyville in a wagon, were incarcerated in the workhouse at the Bedford County seat.

Although Sheriff Williams would not admit it, he was very uneasy about adding these two accused police murderers to his jail. For the last six weeks, Bedford County had been a powder keg of lynching threats after the murder of two of Shelbyville's police officers by the livery stable operator and notorious bootlegger Marion Anderson. Anderson fled the scene of the murders on Halloween night. Before he was captured in early January, there had been no less than two dozen threats made to the sheriff's office that when Anderson was brought to justice, a mob was going to assault the jail and lynch him. Afraid that these threats would be carried out, Williams hastily dispatched Anderson to Nashville for safekeeping on the afternoon of his arrest.

Now they would have to protect two more accused murderers of a policeman, and these two were Black. Additionally, this time, Sheriff Williams would not have the luxury of taking his prisoners to a remote location for safekeeping. Bedford County had paid to transfer Anderson to Nashville and paid the Davidson County Sheriff's office for his incarceration. The sheriff knew there simply would be nothing left in his budget to pay for sequestering Greer and Neal from the rage of the mobs.

The morning following the capture and detention of the two men, a delegation of concerned Bedford County citizens called upon the sheriff in hopes that they might convince him to expedite the judicial procedures by holding a special term of criminal court. They thought that if these men could be brought to trial as soon as possible, some tension and resentment against them could be eliminated.

Williams was not the only one concerned with the threat of violence against the two Negroes. On Monday, February 12th, two days after the arrest, a reporter placed a long-distance phone call from the *Nashville Tennessean* newspaper in Nashville to Sheriff Williams. The reporter asked the sheriff if he feared any retribution toward his prisoners by the citizens of Shelbyville. Williams assured the reporter that as of that night, all was quiet in the city, and there was no danger of mob violence. However, he did admit that there had been murmurs of retaliation during the day. He went on to say that because of what he had heard, he had beefed up the security at the jail.

On Monday, February 12th, two days after the murder, three indictments charging first-degree murder were filed in Shelbyville against Neal, Greer, and the third suspect, Charles Dane Bomar. Bomar was not in custody on the 12th but would be picked up and brought back to Shelbyville from Chattanooga the following day.

The indictment and arrest of Bomar became a contentious matter.

Sometime later, there were conflicting statements from witnesses as to how his actions contributed to the death of the detective. Some said that Bomar helped the brothers force Everson toward the vestibule of the car; some said he was simply in the right place at the wrong time and that he had not participated in any way other than attempting to de-escalate the engagement between the detective and the brothers.

On the night of the murder, 34-year-old Bomar joined Wat Greer and slipped off the train as it slowed its approach into the station at Bell Buckle. Unlike the other two, he eluded being taken into custody that night.

It is unknown how he accomplished it, but by Monday the 12th, he had made his way to Chattanooga. Bomar had friends in the River City who took him in and secreted him away from the law enforcement officers searching for him.

The NC&St.L detectives who investigated the murder speculated that had Bomar not been involved in the altercation, he would not have fled to Chattanooga; instead, he would have exited the train in Wartrace and taken the accommodation train home to Shelbyville.

Working off a tip about where Bomar might be sheltering, NC&St.L Special Agents Alex Barnhill and W.B. Crabtree took a train to Chattanooga to locate Bomar and place him in custody. He was arrested late on the evening of Tuesday night, February 13th, and charged with complicity in the murder of Detective Everson.

Though questioned extensively by the railroad detectives, Bomar remained silent regarding his involvement in the murder. When he did make a statement, he admitted only that he knew it had happened but remained staunch in his story that he was innocent of having anything to do with the death of Everson.

After an intense grilling by law enforcement personnel from the NC&St.L Detective Division and the Bedford County Sheriff's office, the detectives determined that Bomar may not have initiated the altercation. Still, he had nonetheless been a direct participant in the murder. The investigative detectives who intensively interrogated Bomar for several hours were sure that he knew much more about what had happened aboard train No.5 on Saturday than he revealed.

When asked about how much the participants in the murder had been drinking, he stated that Greer and Neal had consumed at least a quart of liquor apiece. He admitted that he, too, had been drinking that night, but he had not finished anywhere close to as much as the other two suspects.

Bomar was taken back to Shelbyville and by Friday was confined in the Bedford County jail along with the other two suspects.

For the second time in ten weeks, Bedford County, Tennessee, a county that had not seen a significant crime in years, had experienced the murder of three police officers. The murders of Officers Henry and Purdy on the previous Halloween night would prove to be an assassination of two of Shelbyville's finest, and now a third law enforcement officer had been murdered within the bounds of the county.

Chapter Three

The First Two Murders: Shelbyville Police Officers Redin G. Purdy and Charles Henry

"When I get out, I am going to kill you!"

Tuesday, October 31, 1911, 3:15 p.m., Shelbyville, Tennessee

Tradition says that on this 1911 Halloween day, the first door-to-door "Guising," a forerunner of Trick-or-Treating, was celebrated in Ontario, Canada. Trick-or-Treating would not come to Shelbyville for a few more years. Instead, the night's festivities would include a community-wide festival of carving jack-o'-lanterns amidst tables adorned with autumn leaves and paper flowers, playing games, bobbing for apples, and donning costumes. Many Shelbyville residents looked forward to attending the Halloween celebration's fun and festivity that evening.

The temperature on this late fall day had risen to an unusually warm 73 degrees. The pleasant weather afforded some of the city's elites a comfortable atmosphere to prepare for the community-wide celebration, which would be held on an empty lot just off the courthouse square. The warm weather would also ensure a massive turnout by the citizens.

At 5:15 p.m., three blocks away from the setup of the Halloween festival, Marion Anderson walked up Depot Street from the Stone and Hobbs livery stables. His destination was Halmantaler's Butcher Shop, a half block west of the livery. The cigarette Anderson had been smoking had burned down so far that if he had taken one more drag from it, it certainly would have burned his lips. Flipping the stub of the cigarette to the curb, he looked ahead and spotted Shelbyville police Officer Hiram H. Rittenberry rounding a corner and heading his way. The officer was also making his way east on Depot toward Halmantaler's Rittenberry was going to the market to purchase meat for his family's next breakfast.

At first, Rittenberry paid no attention to the man approaching him, but that was not the case with Anderson, as he had been watching the officer intently.

As Anderson drew closer to the officer, Rittenberry finally noticed the man. It became immediately evident that Anderson had been drinking heavily. He was stumbling and wobbling, his clothing was tousled, and he was a walking souse.

On October 20th, Shelbyville Officers Rittenberry and his partner Officer Redin G. Purdy had served a public nuisance warrant on Elizabeth M. Baltimore, a woman who, in polite terms, was known to have a soiled reputation. Baltimore had been arrested on several occasions for prostitution, drug use, and drunkenness. The city fathers and the police chief had determined the woman to be a public annoyance—something needed to be done to alleviate the problems she was causing. A warrant declaring her a nuisance was obtained. The officers went to the woman's residence at the Dixie Hotel on the courthouse square at the corner of Martin and Main Streets and had, under the warrant's authority, ordered her to move from the room she was renting. In hopes of reducing the number of encounters the police would have with the woman in the future, the warrant stipulated that she had to move outside the city limits of Shelbyville.

Though Anderson was married and had two sons and two daughters, he had been cohabitating and carrying on a sexual relationship with Elizabeth Baltimore for quite some time.

Upon learning of Baltimore's eviction from her residence, Anderson had been quite bitter that the officers had forced the woman, his love interest, out of town. Shelbyville was a small town. Anderson knew precisely the two officers who had served the eviction warrant on Baltimore. Even though they were serving a warrant in performance of their duties, Marion Anderson took umbrage at the actions of the officers and law enforcement in general. Having been arrested several times by these same two officers who had served the warrant on Mrs. Baltimore, he considered the officers' actions as yet another harassment of himself personally.

Baltimore had complained to Anderson that the officers who served her warrant had gone out of their way to hassle her. Considering Anderson's previous arrest record and run-ins with these same officers, it didn't take much to provoke hard feelings.

Although Anderson had chanced upon Officer Rittenberry on several occasions since the eviction of his female friend, this would be the first time he had encountered him while in such an intoxicated state. He was about to let his inebriation overload his mouth, and it would lead to trouble once again.

Anderson crossed the officer's path as the two men entered the shop. With slurred speech, almost to the point of being incoherent, Anderson started ranting about Rittenberry and his partner Purdy forcing his paramour to vacate her downtown residence.

Rittenberry was confounded for a few seconds, taken aback by this sudden outburst; he did not know what to think of the accusation being leveled at him. Rittenberry could make no sense of what the drunkard was talking about.

Thirty-five-year-old Marion Anderson had an extensive arrest record and was known by the town's police force to often become abusive and belligerent while being arrested. It would not have been unusual for him to formulate a story using his animosity toward the local police officers as a spark to ignite the resentment.

Realizing that things were escalating, Rittenberry tried to relax the situation by calmly talking to him. Anderson would have none of it. In his state of intoxication, he was adamant that the officer had forcefully entered his premises. Anderson became more riled. "I'm gonna make you pay for busting down my door, you son-of-a-bitch." Again, Rittenberry was confused. He had no idea what the drunk was talking about. At no time had he broken down a door to effect an arrest of Anderson. Was he talking about serving the warrant on Baltimore? And even then, no one had broken down a door to make that arrest either. The assailant suddenly reached into the front pocket of his trousers, pulled out a pocketknife, and thrust the knife toward Rittenberry in an attempt to cut him.

In a defensive move, Rittenberry turned to his right and attempted to grab the weapon simultaneously. He missed. Again, the assailant made a swiping motion with the knife. Backing away from the threat, the officer drew his service revolver from its worn leather holster and pointed it toward the man before him. If Anderson had been foolish enough to make one more attempt on the officer's life, Rittenberry would ensure it would be the last mistake this saphead would ever make.

Anderson did charge forward again, and Officer Rittenberry was about to shoot the man when, out of the corner of his eye, he saw Officers Redin Purdy and Charles Henry approaching with guns already drawn. Anderson also saw the other officers arriving and realized he was vastly outnumbered. He backed up a few steps, and the situation de-escalated. The arriving officers made it clear to Anderson that Rittenberry was about to shoot him, and it was in his best interest to raise his hands and drop the knife. Anderson slowly raised his hands but failed to lower the blade until the officers ordered him a second time to do so.

Officer Henry circled behind the disarmed man, pulled his arms roughly up behind, and handcuffed him.

Officers Purdy and Rittenberry took the assailant into custody and did a pat down of the man to make sure he had no more weapons on his person. They started toward the county workhouse at Spring Street and the railroad crossing a few blocks away. As the three men walked away, Anderson's bravado rose again, and he began shouting at the top of his lungs, "You had no right to arrest me. I was minding my own business. When I get out, I am going to kill you!"

The three officers heard the threat but did not understand to whom it was directed … nor did they care.

As the other two officers escorted Anderson toward the jail, Officer Henry stayed behind to take a statement from two citizens who had witnessed the incident.

As quickly as the matter had started, it was now over.

Marion E. Anderson was booked at the workhouse and swiftly brought before a judge in City Court. By this time, Anderson was still intoxicated but a little clearer of head than he had been at the time of his arrest. The judge set a bond of $50 for his drunkenness and for pulling a knife on Officer Rittenberry.

When one of Anderson's friends, J.E. Burris, heard that he had been arrested, he came to the courthouse to see if he could help. After the bond was assessed, his friend paid the $50, and Anderson was released into his custody.

Marion Anderson returned to his residence above the Stone and Hobbs livery stable. His head was now pounding. The threat he had made at his arrest weighed heavily on his mind. Was he serious about wanting to kill someone? That someone was Shelbyville

49

police officer Redin Purdy. Anderson had been arrested dozens of times, but he had had enough this time. His foggy mind and the splitting headache were almost driving him crazy. To him, Officer Purdy was a real bastard. He was sure that Purdy had gone out of his way to arrest him on several occasions. Whether true or not, Anderson had convinced himself of the fact. It was true that Purdy had been the arresting officer at least a dozen times for offenses ranging from drunk and disorderly to bootlegging and gambling. Was it a coincidence? Not to Anderson; this time, he was serious.

As a plot to murder Purdy and Rittenberry churned in his mind, Anderson began running through a checklist of things he would have to carry out to perpetuate the dastardly deed. He knew that the officers would typically walk a routine beat later in the evening, and they generally walked a set pattern as they checked the doors of closed establishments and held a short conversation with the proprietors of those establishments still operating later in the evening. All he would have to do was wait in an alcove along their route, and like flies to his spider, the two men would walk directly into his web of death.

Anderson's presence was unaccounted for during the early evening of that Halloween, but around 7:45 p.m., he returned to his livery driving a buggy pulled by a yellow horse. With him in the buggy were two men, Thomas Jones and J.E. Burris (the man who had made his bond that afternoon.) The three men entered the livery through the large wood sliding door and began to unhitch the horse from the buggy. A couple of minutes later, Searcy Rayburn, Anderson's cousin on his mother's side and an employee of the livery, entered the stables. All three men helped Anderson complete the job of unhitching the horse, and putting away the harness and tack.

Rayburn would later recount that upon his arrival, Marion Anderson was in an almost manic state. He began running through the livery, darting to and fro. He was looking for a saddle to place on the horse. After searching for a few minutes, he could not locate a suitable riding saddle in his livery, so he went next door to Mr. Mullins's livery to find one. Finally finding the subject of his search, he returned to his establishment and asked Burris to help him place the saddle on the horse.

Anderson mounted the horse and set out on a circuitous route through the streets of Shelbyville. His mission was to locate officers Purdy and Rittenberry as they made their patrol rounds. Anderson spotted the two men as they were passing the NC&St.L Depot. He knew that within a few minutes, they would turn west on Depot Street, walk past the livery, and proceed toward the courthouse three blocks away. If he hurried, he could ride back the livery, tie up his yellow mare, and wait for them in the block between Jefferson and Britton Streets.

Looking at the moon as he and his partner patrolled their beat, Officer Henry was reminded of a song on America's hit parade for the last few months, and he began to whistle "Turn Your Light Off, Mister Moon Man."

As the two policemen walked along, Officer Purdy would drop his nightstick from his hand and twirl it by the braided leather lanyard tied to his wrist. Occasionally, with an upward jerk of his wrist, he returned the stick to his hand, catching it by the handle.

On Depot Street, between Jefferson and Britton Streets, there was a vacant building, a poultry and a produce store, and Halmantaler's meat market. As the officers passed each store, they gave the front door handle a swift rattle. Assured that the doors were locked for the night, Officer Henry pointed a beam of light from his flashlight through the windows to illuminate the dark interior of each business.

Because the officers were moving along slowly, checking the security of the businesses, Marion Anderson used this opportunity to close the distance between himself and the police officers stealthily. As soon as he left the livery, he moved diagonally across the street toward the front of the Christian Church on the corner of Depot and Jefferson Streets. He was now across the street from his intended victims and could watch their movements from an undercover position.

Charles Henry switched off the beam of his flashlight and turned west toward the public square. Within moments, he and his partner were directly in front of Halmantaler's.

This time, Anderson would not be arrested … this time, he would not have to get close to the officers to use a knife. All he had to do was wait in the dark and ambush the officers from afar.

The wait was short. Everything was perfect. The moon was at its full brightness. Additionally, only moments later, the officers would be illuminated by the glow of incandescent lighting emanating through the front window of the butcher shop and the street light above. The officers were a well-lit target for a man hiding in the dark.

Marion Anderson raised the pistol in his hand and pointed it at the back of Officer Purdy. Two shots rang out, BANG! BANG! Anderson then pointed his weapon at Officer Henry, and in quick succession, two more shots rang out, BANG! BANG! And it was done.

The four gunshots had hit their marks, and the two officers were down. Both officers lay crumpled on the concrete sidewalk, their life's blood seeping out and mixing with the horse manure, tobacco juice, dirt, and other debris accumulated along the curb of the street.

Jones, Burris, and Rayburn heard the four shots. A few minutes later, Anderson emerged from the darkness, a sinister look on his face and holding a weapon by its barrel. From the way he was holding the gun, all three clearly could see the stock and exposed cylinder of the pistol in the assailant's hand.

Standing in the open door of the livery, Anderson screamed, "I got both of them!" Amazed and confused at first, Jones, Burris, and Rayburn did not know what to make of the outburst they had just heard.

But then all of a sudden, it was clear: the shots, the gun, the look on Anderson's face. The men did not know who had been shot, but it was apparent the man standing in the doorway was the man who had fired the rounds.

Hearing the shots and then her husband's shouting, Tennessee E. (Tennie) Anderson came from their apartment above the livery to see what was happening.

Tennie attempted to approach her husband but to no avail. Mounting the yellow horse, Anderson was in too much of a hurry to pause his getaway. J.E. Burris stepped before the horse to stop its rider from fleeing the scene. A man standing his ground is no match for a full-grown horse with a rider, Burris was brushed aside as Anderson reined the horse into leaving. The men stood and watched as Anderson slapped the horse's haunches and rode away at full gallop to the east of town.

Marshall Waggoner, an employee in the Halmantaler shop, was the first to reach the two officers bleeding out on the sidewalk in front of his store. Officer Purdy was in a half-sitting position, his head resting against the brick wall of the produce goods building adjoining the butcher shop. He had been shot twice, one bullet in the arm and one in the chest. All indications were that he had tried to draw his weapon in defense but never got a shot off at his assailant. Waggoner bent over the downed man to see if he was alive and, if so, if he might aid him in any way. He was breathing, but shallowly; Purdy's blood was ensanguining his uniform and flowing into a pool underneath him.

Officer Henry was located only an arms-length to the left of his partner's limp body. He was face down; his arms had come to rest in a semi-folded position above his waist. Gravely wounded, he had sustained what appeared to be two bullet wounds. Waggoner discovered that the officer was still breathing, though very shallowly.

Doctor T.R. Ray, a local physician, was located and summoned to the scene. Upon his arrival, he determined that Officer Purdy had sustained a bullet wound entering his body through his left arm and exiting just under his right. A second shot, this one most likely fatal, was located in the center mass of the chest and had entered his heart. It was evident that Officer Purdy had already perished from the gunshots, but Officer Henry was still alive, though barely. Doctor Ray immediately started lifesaving procedures in an attempt to keep Officer Henry from death. A farm wagon parked near the ambush site was summoned, and at the doctor's request, the officer was transported to his office. Although Doctor Ray worked feverishly, he could not save the man. Officer Henry, a gunshot wound chest high in the center of his uniform and one just above his waistline, died from his wounds at 10:10 p.m., some 40 minutes after being gunned down in the street.

At 10:00 a.m. the following day, County Coroner William G. Hight concluded an inquest and charged Marion E. Anderson, a citizen of Shelbyville, with two counts of murder. At the same time, three blocks away, the Shelbyville Board of Aldermen met and voted to offer the amount of $250 to anyone who would bring the person of Marion Anderson to the office of the Bedford County Sheriff's office.

Later in the day, several of Shelbyville's more prosperous citizens met to discuss how they might help in bringing justice to the families of the slain men. So enraged were they by the slaying of these highly regarded law enforcement officers, they raised another $250 for the capture of Anderson.

Officer Purdy and Officer Henry were well known in the Shelbyville community. Redin Purdy was not only a respected officer but also, for the last six years, the superintendent of the Bedford County Home for the Poor. He said serving in this non-salaried position was his Christian duty.

Left behind by his death were his wife, Belle, and two married daughters.

Charles Henry was a native of nearby Bell Buckle. He left behind his wife, Laura, and five young children, two of whom were suffering from typhoid fever.

When word of the murders reached Nashville, Tennessee Governor Ben Hooper increased the reward by adding another $500 to the $500 already approved by the Shelbyville aldermen and the citizens. Another $100 was offered by Officer Henry's two brothers. The reward now stood at $1,100.

On the night of the murders, Anderson was seen around 9:30 p.m. on the outskirts of Shelbyville, as he rode "hell-bent for leather" out Horse Mountain Road toward Wartrace. It was not an accident; this was also the road on which Anderson's paramour, Elizabeth Baltimore, lived. Baltimore had moved in with her brother after being forced to vacate her town apartment by the Shelbyville police department earlier in the month.

At around 10:30 p.m., the fugitive was then seen 13 miles away from Shelbyville near Haley's Station, a whistle-stop on the Nashville-to-Chattanooga tracks of the NC&St.L Railway. The sighting near

Haley's Station immediately drew speculation that the suspect must be trying to make his way toward Coffee County. Anderson's father and several other relatives lived in Coffee County, just over the line from Bedford County. It seemed that the fugitive was trying to make it to the shelter of his family.

That speculation seemed to be confirmed when he was seen in the tiny hamlet of Cortner in the early hours of Wednesday morning. (This sighting may have been in error since Anderson later proved to have stopped at the home of Walter Hickerson around 11:00 p.m. It was never explained why Anderson stopped at the home of Mr. Hickerson. Hickerson was not a friend or even an acquaintance of the defendant. It may have been that Anderson simply stopped because the lateness of the hour and that Hickerson's farm was convenient.

At around 7:00 a.m. Wednesday, acting on the report of the sighting in Cortner, Bedford County Sheriff Williams and a posse of about 20 deputized men, plus several citizens from Shelbyville and Bedford County who went on the hunt on their own, headed toward Cortner looking for the suspect. Shortly afterward, Captain Allen and bloodhounds from the sheriff's office joined the search.

By around 2:00 p.m., those combing the countryside had grown to nearly 300 men. That many men joining the hunt could be attributed to two factors. First, some thought they might get part of the $1,100 reward (more than $27,000 in 2023 dollars) raised earlier in the day. Second, the Wednesday morning *Nashville Tennessean* would sum up the feelings of many of the Shelbyville citizens when it reported: "Shelbyville has never had in her 100 years' existence a tragedy that has so stirred up her citizens." So incensed was the populace of Bedford County that when these men located the suspect, it could be assured that a lynching would take place. These people were certainly not going to allow the murder of one of their own to go on without swift and sure justice.

Fortunately, Sheriff Williams' fear that he would have to defend the suspect from what undoubtedly was become an unruly mob did not materialize.

A break in the search occurred late on Wednesday, November 1st when the yellow horse Anderson had used in his escape was found. It was still saddled and tethered to a tree on the outskirts of Normandy, Tennessee. Anderson after arriving at Walter Hickerson's place, had told Hickerson to set the horse free. Hickerson, not wanting the horse to get hurt or lost, instead secured it in a place where it would be found.

When the horse was located, the members of the sheriff's posse expressed excitement. The searchers assumed that Anderson could not be far from his horse and that the fugitive's arrest was imminent.

Locating the horse was a boon for those who were truly serious about the hunt. For others, not so much so. As shadows fell and damp darkness set in, many of the 300 men had had enough and returned to their farm wagons or mounted their horses to make their way back toward home. The excitement of the day's hunt had not produced any more clues concerning the murderer's whereabouts. While the searchers were tracking back and forth near Cortner, Marion Anderson was able to elude the scrutiny of trained law enforcement officers, bloodhounds, and a mob of private citizens set on a lynching vendetta by simply holding his position in a corncrib in Normandy. Marion Anderson was not found that day; in fact, he eluded capture for over two months.

Anderson avoided capture for weeks because he kept changing his hideaway. He had four sisters and nine brothers living within a 15-mile radius of Shelbyville. During his time as a fugitive, Anderson moved from one sibling's home to another, ensuring he did not remain in any one location for an extended time. With each move, he hid in the tall grasses surrounding the farms and scouted the area, ensuring no law enforcement agents were waiting to spring a trap on him as he moved from hideout to hideout.

Constantly in pursuit, the law enforcement officers of Bedford County did not allow Anderson to rest while he was on the run. Three Bedford County law officers considered it their utmost duty to bring justice to the families of the slain policemen. Those three men were former Bedford County Sheriff W.G. Rucker, Detective Robert Corbitt (a Chattanooga private detective hired by Officer Henry's brothers), and Bedford County Sheriff James Williams. These three worked doggedly, keeping pressure on the suspect to the point that Anderson would later comment that "those damned detectives were on every hill so thick that I could not get away, and finally, I had to give myself up."

Detective Corbitt went door-to-door posing as a picture book salesman when, in fact, he was canvassing the areas he was visiting looking for the suspect. As time passed, information came into the sheriff's office of sightings, but the information did not lead to the capture of the subject of their search.

The last week of December, when a break in the search for the alleged murderer had not materialized, and it seemed that nothing new was on the horizon, Sheriff Williams stepped up the pressure. Elizabeth Baltimore, the attractive 32-year-old paramour of the wanted man, was taken into custody with the pretense of protecting her as a material witness.

The truth was that Williams was not trying so much to protect her as he was to lock her away, hoping to extract information from her or, more to the point, to use her as a pawn in a high-stakes game of finding Anderson's hiding place. After a little over a week of confinement, Detective Corbitt visited her in her cell. In exchange for her freedom, he wanted her to give him information. Baltimore, tired of her confinement, confided to the detective that just after the events of that Halloween night, Anderson had come to her house and hidden there for a short while. Afraid that the authorities would be looking for him at her house, he told her that he planned on crossing into Coffee County, where he intended to hide, alternating at homes of his relatives.

Tuesday, January 2, 1912, 3:00 p.m., Fairfield, Tennessee

By mid-morning on Tuesday, January 2nd, Sheriff Williams had combined the information from Elizabeth Baltimore with another substantiated tip relayed to Detective Corbitt and narrowed his search for the fugitive. The information indicated that the escapee might be hiding near the community of Fairfield in Coffee County, about 12 miles from the place of the murder.

Detective Corbitt's pressure on Elizabeth Baltimore for information was the breakthrough the searchers had been looking for. The tip was reliable for Williams and substantiated what the sheriff had surmised. The sheriff was pretty sure that Paul B. Myers, a friend and attorney for the fugitive, had been in communication with Anderson since the night of the murders. It seemed likely that he had been using Myers's house as a hideout as part of his rotation.

Armed with the new information, the sheriff summoned a group of men to form a posse. Drawn together were Constable James Taylor, Sam Thompson and Will Hastings (two Shelbyville policemen), and Walter Jones, who was sworn in as a deputy for this occasion.

Arriving at the Myers home a little after 2:00 p.m., the sheriff quickly realized he was joining a party of law officers already at the house. Already on the scene were former sheriff W.G. Rucker and one of his men, R.J. Whittborne, who, like the sheriff, had been tracking the fugitive for weeks.

W.G. Rucker had been a deputy sheriff of Bedford County for eight years and then had served as high sheriff for an additional four. He and Sheriff Williams were now candidates in a heated race against one another for the position of county sheriff. Arresting the murderer of Officers Purdy and Henry would go a long way toward securing either candidate the office for the next four years.

The competition between the two would account for the differing narratives of Marion Anderson's arrest in a Nashville paper.

Sheriff Williams gave an account of the arrest to the *Nashville Tennessean* and the *Nashville American*. Printed in the January 4, 1912 edition, his statement read:

> I was in my office around 11:00 this morning when information came from a source I cannot disclose stating that Marion Anderson was at Mr. Paul Myers' home. I took four other men with me, and we proceeded to the Myers' house in Coffee County.

He continued his narrative:

> Upon our arrival ... we went up the hill to the house; I ordered my men to surround it. Two went to each side, and I took the front. Paul Myers was standing on the front porch of his house. When we got close to the house, he stepped off the porch to the front yard and then ran to the smokehouse at the rear of the house. I called to him, and when he came up, I stated my business and asked him who was in the house. He laughed and didn't say anything. I told him he might as well tell me; if he didn't, I would find out for myself. He then stated that (Sheriff) W.G. Rucker and R.J. Whittborne were in the house and that Marion Anderson was locked in the smokehouse.
>
> I told him I had an arrest warrant for Anderson and wanted him. He unlocked the door to the smokehouse, and I took custody of the

> fugitive. When we entered the house, I found Rucker and Whittborne in the sitting room, which had been refitted into a bedroom. I told the two men that I had placed Marion Anderson under arrest and that he was now in my custody. At that point, Whittborne pulled some papers from his pockets and said that Anderson was already under arrest under those papers. I asked to see the documents. I needed to find out who made those out. I learned that no official had signed them and thus had no arrest validity. I then drew my warrant from my jacket and read it to the arrestee, placing Anderson officially under arrest.
>
> Anderson's only request was to let him see his wife and children, which we granted (after returning toward Shelbyville). As we left for Nashville in the automobile, he did not have an overcoat, so his 15-year-old son pulled off his coat and threw it around his father's shoulders.

Talking to the same newspapers, former Sheriff W.G. Rucker gave a slightly differing account that portrayed him as the one who had captured Anderson.

Rucker's statement went as follows:

> I found Anderson between Fairfield and Wartrace about 12 miles from Shelbyville. (The arrest was) "done between the early hours of midnight and 2:00 a.m. on Tuesday the 2nd." He said, "He had been tipped off that Anderson had been trying to see his wife and that we had laid for him." When asked where he captured the prisoner, he said, "(The arrest) was made in the house." Still, as Mr. Myers objected to his name being put on the paper, the ex-sheriff said, "It was done in the house of a friend of Anderson's." When asked the friend's name, Rucker said he did not know it.

He reported placing Anderson in Myers's smokehouse for safekeeping until other arrangements could be made.

These two accounts indicated that former Sheriff Rucker had made the initial arrest and that he and his partner, R.J. Whittborne, were in Paul Myers's house, patiently waiting for the current sheriff to come and take custody of the arrestee.

Word of Anderson's arrest spread quickly back to Shelbyville. As the suspect was being transported back to town, word was received that a group of hostiles was beginning to assemble near the jail, and it was assumed that these men would attempt to take Anderson from the deputies to lynch him.

Sheriff Williams immediately surmised that attempting to jail the prisoner in the Bedford County jail would not be prudent. The sheriff understood that trying to hold Anderson in Shelbyville this night would culminate in a fight for the life of his prisoner.

Anderson would have to be served the mittimus and be formally charged with the crime of capital murder. Still so afraid was Sheriff Williams that a hostile mob might try to seize control of his prisoner, he summoned Squire B.R. Whitthorne, a local magistrate, to come to a location outside of Shelbyville rather than attempt to take Anderson into town. Creating a temporary courtroom inside a roadside general store, the magistrate committed Anderson to jail without bail and set the date of January 15th for trial.

After the magistrate established a court date for the defendant, the sheriff called Nashville long distance and facilitated arrangements to bring Anderson to the state capitol for safekeeping in the Davidson County jail.

A little after 4:00 p.m., a borrowed Model T Ford (in 1911 parlance, known as a "machine") containing the accused, his attorney Paul Myers, current Sheriff Williams, former Sheriff Rucker, and one Bedford County deputy departed Shelbyville heading toward Nashville. Suspecting there might be some reprisal, Sheriff Williams kept a careful eye along the roadway until they passed from Bedford into Rutherford County and were motoring toward Murfreesboro.

The trip to Nashville turned out to be an adventurous one.

When the car reached the outskirts of Murfreesboro, a front tire on the Tin-Lizzie went flat. After a brief stop, the air in the tire was restored using a hand pump located in the car for just such a purpose. After the inflation was completed, the vehicle and its occupants proceeded. Only a few minutes later, another one of the tires succumbed to the roughness of the road, and it, too, went flat. Too damaged to be refilled with air this time, the spare tire from the car's back bumper was used as a replacement for the flat. After that flat was replaced, the group proceeded toward Nashville. When they reached the hamlet of Brooklyn about 12 miles south of Nashville, the same tire that had gone flat outside of Murfreesboro completely disintegrated, flinging chunks of the rubber tire in all directions. With the spare already put to use earlier, there was no auxiliary tire to make repairs.

The sheriff attempted to drive further on just three tires and the wood rim of the fourth. After proceeding for a mile, it became apparent that the rough condition of the hard-paned road made trying to advance fruitless. Riding on the rim, and what was left of the tire was beating senseless the occupants of the Ford.

Sheriff Williams located a phone and made a long-distance call to the Tennessee Automobile Company in Nashville. The automobile service dispatched a car, and the party was ferried to the Davidson County jail, arriving just after 9:00 p.m.

What should have been a two-hour trip had taken over five hours to complete.

The arrival of the notorious murderer of two police officers was anticipated after word was received that he was being shuttled to Nashville for safekeeping.

News of their travel preceded them. The long-distance phone lines in

Middle Tennessee were ablaze for hours as the Model T made its way toward Nashville. As soon as the automobile passed a point along the route, someone would call Nashville to report the caravan's progress.

Upon the automobile's arrival, a local photographer was waiting on the sidewalk just outside the jail. The photographer, M.W. Wilson from the *Nashville Banner*, snapped a candid photo of the suspect and his captors as they exited the car. A few minutes later, inside the building, the same photographer asked Anderson whether he could take another photograph. Anderson was a physical wreck, exhausted from his time on the run. His face was drawn and haggard. His feet were swollen to twice their normal size, and he was dressed in three pairs of mud-covered overalls, two blue shirts, a floppy felt hat, muddy work boots, and the brown overcoat his son had thrown over his shoulders as they were leaving Fairfield. He refused to allow his photo to be snapped for a second time. He considered himself somewhat of a "Dapper Dan," and he told the photographer he would gladly allow a second photo to be taken after he obtained some clean clothes and was allowed to shave the now two-inch-long beard that had been growing since he had been on the run. Vanity was one of Marion Anderson's more essential traits.

The second photograph was never taken.

A Davidson County sheriff's clerk was handed a copy of the mittimus issued by the Bedford County magistrate charging Anderson with the murder of the two officers. The clerk entered on the jail registration blotter that the prisoner before him was a 33-year-old White man, 5 feet 9 inches tall, 155 pounds, with coffee-colored eyes, a semi-ruddy complexion, and terrible teeth. (Anderson had a large overbite, and his two front teeth were so severely decayed that one had almost rotted away.)

A *Nashville Tennessean* and *Nashville American* newspaper reporter was waiting inside the jail. With a pencil and notebook in hand, the reporter called for an interview with the sheriff and the suspect. Anderson granted an interview with the correspondent. When questioned about his arrest, the suspect stated,

> "I was walking along the road between Wartrace and Shelbyville at around 1:00 a.m. when I was stopped at gunpoint by former Sheriff Rucker, who demanded me to identify myself. He then asked, 'Is that you, Anderson?' I admitted that I was he. Rucker placed me under arrest and took me back to Shelbyville."

(This statement is in direct contrast with the statements made by Sherriff Williams and ex-Sheriff Rucker.) Anderson continued his statement by saying,

> "I am innocent of the crime with which I am charged, and I may add that my false accusers who have caused my arrest have my sympathy. When a full investigation of the heinous crime committed is made, I will be fully relieved of guilt in this matter."

The article appearing in the following day's paper reported that Anderson had eluded capture from October 31st to January 2nd by moving from hiding place to hiding place and that it had been only through the dogged pursuit of officers like Detective Corbitt and ex-Sheriff Rucker that an arrest had finally been accomplished. Sheriff Williams gave most of the credit to Corbitt and himself by saying, "Corbitt and I made it so hot on Anderson that Paul Myers induced him to give himself up." He continued, "In my opinion, this is why Anderson was found in Myers' smokehouse."

Williams said that Anderson told him after the capture, "Those damned detectives were on every hill so thick, he couldn't get away, and he had to give himself up."

When asked by the reporter about what he thought of Anderson's statement that he "had been falsely charged with the shooting of the two officers," Sheriff Williams said, "He is guilty, and on the day of trial, I will prove it."

Friday, January 5, 1912, 4:00 p.m., Davidson County Jail, Nashville, Tennessee

So enthralled was the public by the story about the murders in Shelbyville that a reporter from the *Nashville Tennessean* interviewed Anderson again on the 5th of January. During the interview, Anderson—who seemed to be in high spirits and not overly concerned with his present predicament—was questioned about his whereabouts during his disappearance. He refused to answer the reporter's question, deflecting instead to professing his innocence in the murder of the officers and saying that his innocence would be proven at the time of his preliminary hearing.

At this point, Anderson went on the defense with his interrogator. "It seems hard," said Anderson, "that a man should be hunted from place to place like a wild beast and be separated from his family because of the enmity of a few unscrupulous men." He went on to say, "My wife was worried to death all the time that I was out, fearing that at any moment she might hear that someone having shot me for the sake of the reward that was offered."

Changing his point of emphasis, he then suggested, "The people who had offered the $1,000 should use the money to track down the real murderer rather than to have used it to track me down."

Anderson went on to construct an alternate theory about who had killed Officers Henry and Purdy. He told the reporter that he and the two slain officers were such good friends that if, during his time of hiding, he had gone to any of the two men's relatives' homes, they would have given him food and would not have turned him away. Anderson proclaimed that he had enemies in the Shelbyville community, and that because he has enemies, those enemies had murdered the officers because he was a friend of theirs. The prisoner said that it had just been his luck that he had not been with the officers at the time of their murder. He went on to say that he had intended to turn himself in to the authorities for his own protection, but when he discovered that a posse had formed and that a $1,000 bounty had been placed on his head, he decided to flee for his safety. He contended that the same enemies had murdered the two officers and had gotten the $1,000 "dead or alive" bounty put on Anderson's head.

Anderson refused to answer when asked who these enemies were and why they would have such a vendetta against him, saying only that the truth would become evident when the trial started on January 15th.

So sure had Anderson been that he would get away with these murders during his time on the run, he had contemplated writing Governor Hooper a letter declaring his innocence and explaining to him point by point what had happened and asking the governor for protection.

The letters were never written.

In a jailhouse interview with a reporter with the *Nashville Tennessean* on January 6th, the self-assured Anderson handed the reporter a prepared written statement about the murders with which he was being charged. Additionally, he gave an oral report to the reporter when questions were asked about the events of October 31st.

In the written statement, the accused murderer stated in part,

> "Contrary to rumors I had heard before my capture and what I have read in the newspapers, and to fears created by those rumors and papers, I desire to state that I was treated as kindly and considerately as I could

or should have been by my captors and when I was turned over to Sheriff Williams of Bedford County, I had longed and grieved to see my good wife and my dear children and though captured before I could. I was permitted by (the) generous sheriff to visit and to greet them—a favor of all favors to me and to which privilege I am grateful above all gratitude to him. Then, as was his duty and manly desire, he and others brought me safely to Nashville.

"I want to say that jailers Lowry and Bragg, who permitted me as much privilege as any others here, treated me most kindly and considerately. My cell is light, comfortable, well-ventilated, and my food is abundant and wholesome. I have been treated well by my jailers here in Nashville."

The preliminary hearing was initially set for trial on January 15th but was continued until February 1, 1912. The delay in setting the date for the hearing also delayed Marion Anderson's return to Shelbyville. He would remain in the Davidson County Jail until he was finally returned on January 31st.

Chapter Four

The Marion Anderson Preliminary Hearing
"O Daddy, O Daddy, what made you do that?"

The Preliminary Hearing

Thursday, February 1, 1912, 9:00 a.m., Shelbyville, Tennessee

On Tuesday, January 31st, Sheriff Williams and deputies McCrory and Davis drove back to Nashville to collect Anderson, who needed to be transported back to Shelbyville for his preliminary hearing the following morning. Anderson vigorously protested the move because he had wanted to wait until the following Thursday when several of his friends would be on hand to give him a rousing "homecoming." And perhaps he was afraid to be brought back to Shelbyville because he feared being taken from the jail by a mob of hostiles. Although he never mentioned this, it had to be in his mind.

Meanwhile, every train navigating the eight-mile branch of the Nashville Chattanooga & St. Louis Railway from Wartrace seemed to overflow with people making their way to Shelbyville for the hearing. It was estimated that well over 1,200 new faces were seen in the city for what was sure to be something to behold.

Among those to arrive by train were the defendant's three brothers. All three were residents of Coffee County, and it had been at their homes that Marion had hidden at some point while on the run from authorities. Also on the train was Elizabeth M. Baltimore, the defendant's mistress. Her return was under subpoena by the defense. It was supposed that she would testify that she and the defendant were in the middle of a romantic tryst when the shots rang out, thus giving Anderson an alibi for the time the murders were committed. It was not reported whether Tennie, the defendant's wife, who still resided in the city, was there to greet Elizabeth as she stepped from the late evening train.

By noon, over a thousand persons had filled the courthouse to overflowing. The choice seats in the courtroom were filled hours before the mid-day starting time. Those unable to find seating in the courtroom flowed out into the hallway and down the stairwell, anticipating at least getting a glimpse of the defendant as he was ushered into the courthouse. Those not lucky enough to have gained a seat in the courtroom or were able to fit somewhere in the rest of the building, had pushed through the courthouse to line the streets of Shelbyville, sometimes two or three deep, as onlookers tried to catch sight of the infamous murderer as he was being paraded from his holding cell to court.

At around 12:30 p.m., Sheriff Williams began the two-block move of the prisoner from the jail to the courthouse and then to the Circuit Court courtroom on the second floor. Accompanying the sheriff were six of the sheriff's deputies. Williams was taking no chances that a mob of citizens might take things into their own hands and circumvent the legal process that would play out in the courtroom. A large contingent of those who had taken their place along the roadway between the jail and the courthouse pushed their way onto the grounds, and a few added to those already overflowing the hallways inside.

Sheriff Williams had some difficulties pushing through the crowds, but finally, the defendant was delivered to the table where his defense attorneys were waiting. In a smart pinstripe suit, Marion Anderson took his place at the table between lead attorney J.D. Murphree and co-council Thomas R. Myers. [4]

Across the aisle from the defense table was the one for the county's prosecutors. The county's top two prosecutors, Attorney General

---

[4] Paul B. Myers, at whose house the defendant had been hiding, was the son and law partner of the defense attorney Thomas Myers.

Coldwell and Attorney General Thomas N. Greer, were present to prosecute the case for the state.

Many of Anderson's friends and relatives had found a place in the courtroom directly behind the defendant's table. They were there to give moral support. The defendant's father sat at one end of the defense table, and his brothers stationed themselves directly behind him.

The overflow crowd nestled in, straining their necks as they attempted to get the best view of the proceedings about to begin. Presiding Magistrate J.P. Brantley gaveled the hearing into session at 1:00 p.m. on Thursday, February 1st.

When a list of witnesses was called for, Mr. Myers stood and announced that, at least for the moment, the defense had no witnesses to call. This was a shock to those in the courtroom who had no reservations in thinking that the defendant would take the opportunity to testify in his own defense. After all, Anderson, on the night of his arrest, had boasted to the newspaper reporters in Nashville how he would prove his innocence at the first opportunity he was given to do so. Those who knew Anderson, whether friends or foes, had crowded the courtroom to witness the spectacle of the egotistical defendant taking his chance to tell his side of what had happened on that Halloween night. But those who had come to see the circus were sorely disappointed. Anderson's attorneys convinced him this was not the time or place to take the stand.

The reading of the warrant against the defendant was waived, and at that point, the defense attorneys asked that the rule be enforced. The rule stated that if a person were to be a witness in the trial, he or she would need to be dismissed from the courtroom so as not to be influenced by the testimony of any of the other witnesses in the case.

At this point, Magistrate Brantley told the prosecution to call its first witness. Assistant Attorney General Greer rose and said in a loud, clear voice, "The prosecution calls Mr. Searcy M. Rayburn to the stand."

Upon questioning, Rayburn related that he had lived in Manchester, Tennessee, until a few months before the night of October 31st and that the defendant had offered him a job at the livery on Depot Street and he had taken the position.

"Mr. Rayburn, were you at your place of employment, the livery stables, on the evening of October 31st?" the attorney asked.

"Yes, I was."

"And on the evening of the 31st, did you have an encounter with the defendant, Mr. Anderson?"

"Yes."

"In your own words, please tell us what happened to the defendant," Greer prompted.

"Well, Marion came into the livery driving a buggy pulled by a yellow mare," Rayburn continued.

"And about what time was the time that he arrived?"

"About 8:30."

"Go on, please, Mr. Rayburn. How would you describe the defendant's frame of mind? Was he mad? Did he seem upset?"

"I would say he was somewhat upset. Upon his arrival, Marion asked me to unhitch the horse from the buggy, which I did. He then told me to find a saddle, as he wanted to tack up the animal for riding. I told him we did not have a saddle in the livery because I had rented the last one out earlier in the afternoon. When I told him there was no saddle in the stables, he became more irritated than he had been."

"What do you mean more irritated?"

"Well, I thought he was already in a very foul mood. He was ranting about being unjustly arrested and vowing to get even with the police officers who had arrested him earlier in the day. He became even more upset when I told him we did not have a saddle."

"Go on, Mr. Rayburn. Please tell us what happened next," prompted the attorney.

"Knowing that there was no saddle in our livery, Marion went down the street to the Mullin's livery, and there, he thought he could borrow a saddle. Anyway, he came back carrying a saddle. When he returned, I and the two other men in the livery helped the defendant place it and the rest of the tack on the horse. Anderson then mounted the horse and rode away. About 30 minutes later, he rode back to our livery, walked the horse to Depot Street, and tied the animal's reins to the front door. I asked him if he wanted me to unsaddle the horse. He said no, then told everyone within earshot not to bother the animal."

Rayburn said the defendant disappeared into the dark toward the courthouse square. Under direct examination, he was unable to say precisely what happened next. All he could say was that within several minutes after Anderson had disappeared into the darkness, he heard the report of a firearm. Rayburn said that no more than a minute or two after hearing the gunfire, the defendant returned to the stables quickly.

"Anderson was frantic upon his return. He was …"

"Did you see a gun at this point?" interrupted Greer.

"No, not at this point," continued the witness, "though I could see that Marion had something in his hand. I could not make out what it was he was holding."

"How far were you away from the defendant at this time?"

"I could not have been more than three or four feet from him."

"Did you ever see a weapon of any kind?"

"Yes, a few moments later, I realized that the item I had seen in his hand was the stock and cylinder of a revolver. He was holding the pistol by its barrel. It seemed strange that he was holding the pistol backward from how someone would normally hold a gun, but that was what he was doing."

"Proceed," said Greer.

"He shouted, 'I got both of them,'" Rayburn said.

Rayburn went on to testify he was a bit perplexed about the meaning of this outburst. Rayburn said he heard what he thought to have been four shots just before Anderson came running back to the stables. Again, he stated that in the heat of the moment, he did not fully connect the shots, the outburst by Marion, and the sight of a pistol in his hand as being a part of what had just happened. It was only after he learned that a shooting had occurred a couple of blocks away that he began to understand.

At this point, the prosecuting attorney took his seat.

Defense attorney Thomas B. Myers rose and approached the witness. "Now, Mr. Rayburn, what time do you say that my client, Mr. Anderson, arrived at the livery in the buggy?"

"About 8:30. He came in driving the buggy pulled by that pale-yellow mare."

"And about what time did you say he rode away?"

"Marion came in but then left again. He returned at around 9:00, maybe 9:05. This was when he tied the horse to the front door of the livery."

Attorney Myers then asked if he knew where the defendant had gone between the time he came in driving the buggy and his return on horseback.

Rayburn answered by saying, "I did not."

On further examination, Myers asked if he had seen Anderson with a gun before the night of the shooting, the night of the 31st.

"I knew that Marion owned a gun, but I do not recall ever seeing him carrying it."

"Did you see him with a gun when he first arrived at the livery that night?"

"I did not see a gun either of the first two times he came into the stable that night, but as I told Mr. Greer a minute ago, I did see one when he came back on foot just before he rode away. He might have had one earlier, but it was dark, and I might have missed it."

Rayburn added that when Anderson mounted the horse to ride away, he was only about three or four feet from the defendant, and this was another reason he was able to see the pistol in his hand.

Attorney Myers then asked who was in the stable at the time Marion Anderson returned on foot after the shots were heard.

"Doctor Odum was on the first floor when Marion returned to the stable. Doctor Odum had arrived at our office looking for Jockey Joe Smith, who had been there earlier. A moment later, Mrs. Anderson came down to the livery from her upstairs apartment."

In what turned out to be an unsolicited utterance from the witness, Rayburn said, "I remember seeing the barrel of the pistol in his hand. He was wearing a light coat and a wide-brim hat."

Again, without being prompted, the witness added that as the defendant was about to ride away, Anderson's wife, hearing the commotion in the street, ran out from their apartment to the middle of the street screaming, "O Daddy, O Daddy, what made you do that?" Mrs. Anderson's outburst was in response to the defendant having just yelled out that he had shot the two officers.

At this point, tempers flared. Attorney Myers accused the witness of perjuring himself. He accused Rayburn of willfully testifying to events he had not mentioned during his appearance at the coroner's hearing two months before. When asked if he had withheld any testimony, Rayburn replied that he had not. To the best of his knowledge, he said, he had stated nothing contradictory to anything he had stated previously.

The argument between the two attorneys continued. The prosecution attorney objected to the line of questioning the defense attorney was hurling at the witness. Then, the defense counsel reiterated that

Rayburn was attempting to introduce additional testimony at trial that had yet to be stated before the coroner at that inquest.

When the questioning by Thomas Myers continued, Rayburn responded again that he had answered all the questions directed to him at the coroner's inquest. He said that to the best of his knowledge, he had not reported anything at the preliminary hearing he had not reported at the time of the inquest, or he had not stated anything contrary at the hearing from that which he had said in the courtroom today.

To catch the witness in a lie, or at least throw him off his game, the defense attorney asked Rayburn if it were not true that he had been offered $100 to testify against his client.

Prosecuting attorney Coldwell immediately rose to his feet to object to the inference from Myers.

Judge Brantley sustained Coldwell's objection, and the testimony proceeded. Realizing that Myers had been called out on this question, Rayburn denied the allegation.

Attorney Myers then asked Rayburn what he had done with the money given to him to be used as bail money for the defendant. The witness said instead of using the money for bail, he had given it to Paul Myers, the questioner's son, to pay legal fees.

There is an old adage that an attorney should not ask a question to which he does not already know the answer. Attorney Myers had violated this principle, and it had backfired immensely; the explanation Rayburn gave caught Myers off guard. Instead of shedding a dark light on Rayburn by making it look like he had inappropriately used money entrusted to him for bail for personal gain, Myers had been made to look rather foolish when Rayburn said, "Well, sir, I used the money to pay your legal fees because you insisted that your fees be paid in advance of you taking the case."

At that point, the audience in the courtroom broke into laughter.

"Mr. Rayburn, have you had contact with our client since the 31st of October?"

"No, the last time I saw Mr. Anderson was the night he rode away from the livery."

No other questions were asked of this witness, and Rayburn was excused from the witness stand.

The next person to be called to testify was farmer Walter D. Hickerson of Normandy. On questioning by the prosecution attorney Greer about what he knew of the matter before the court, Mr. Hickerson related that he was a resident of the county and that he lived near Normandy, Tennessee. He stated that the defendant had arrived at his house riding a yellow mare around 10:30 p.m. on Halloween night. He said that both the horse and rider were sweating after what must have been a hard ride. He went on to say that Anderson had requested shelter for the night. Although the hour was late, the request was granted, subject to Anderson sleeping in the corncrib beside the house.

The following day, the defendant asked Hickerson to purchase firearm cartridges if he went to town in Normandy. "Did you purchase those cartridges, Mr. Hickerson?" Greer asked.

"No, I did not go into town until after Mr. Anderson was gone," responded Hickerson.

"Did you ask the defendant why he wanted you to purchase those cartridges?"

"Yes, I did ask, and he told me that some policemen had roughed him up after he was arrested and that he had had some trouble with them."

Hickerson went on with his testimony, "Anderson left my farm that evening on foot. He left the horse behind saying, 'In the light of the bright moon that night, someone might recognize the animal,' or something like that."

The attorney asked, "So what happened to the horse?"

"It is my understanding that Sheriff Williams found it a short time after I tied it to a tree near my farm."

During the hearing, defense attorney Myers called five witnesses to the stand despite initially stating that no witnesses would be called. The prosecution had subpoenaed all five witnesses but had not called upon them to testify. Four of the five, C.L. Nichols, Horace Shearing, Will Winn, and R.A. Taylor, each stated they had no knowledge about the case and were dismissed without testifying.

Of those five, only James Sheppardson provided testimony. He was the person who had sold the yellow mare to the defendant in mid-October. Both attorneys questioned him about the horse's endurance and stamina. Sheppardson mentioned that Anderson had also asked him the same question on the day of the purchase. Anderson wanted to know if the horse was capable of running 30 miles without getting exhausted.

After it was learned that Anderson had sought to purchase a horse capable of making such a long and demanding run, some in the courtroom began to wonder if he had been calculating murder and had anticipated the need for a strong getaway animal as part of his plan. And with that, the testimony in the hearing ended. Magistrate Brantley bound the matter over for trial without reservation.

Counselor Murphree asked for bail, but the judge denied the request. The trial was set for the April term of the Circuit Court. The prosecutors and the defense attorneys agreed upon a new trial date of May 27, 1912.

The hearing had ended abruptly. Of the twelve or fifteen witnesses summoned to testify for the prosecution, only three had been called. The real surprise had been that the defense had also called five of those twelve for their purposes.

Anderson had completed his first day of the hearing. He had not, as he had promised he would in that January interview with a *Nashville Tennessean* reporter, proved his innocence. On the advice of his attorneys, he had made no statement at all. Instead, he kept a keen eye on what happened during the trial. He sat quietly at the defense table, taking notes and whispering something in Attorney Myers' ear from time to time as though he had been directing them on strategy and the course of action he wanted the counselors to take.

Sheriff Williams rushed to the defense table to take control of his prisoner as soon as the hearing ended. His job was challenging, as many of Anderson's friends swarmed the table to offer handshakes and words of encouragement. With so many people around him, the sheriff's deputies had to wedge their way through the crowd to gain possession of the man.

Sheriff Williams now faced a troublesome situation. He would have to move the prisoner back down the street to the security of the jail.

About three thousand people were estimated to be in town to witness the hearing, and not all of them were friends of the defendant.
An estimated 500 men followed the sheriff's party as they left the courthouse to walk to the jail just over two blocks away. Of this group, approximately half were friends of the defendant. His

friends followed in case trouble was started by anyone who might try to take the prisoner by force. Though some were pushing and shoving, and loud taunts were heard, the jail was reached without any significant disturbances.

That evening, to ensure there were no problems at the jail, an extra heavy guard of deputies was assigned to secure the perimeter.

Chapter Five

A Lynching in Town

Friday, February 16, 1912, 6:00 p.m., Shelbyville, Tennessee

Dave Neal and Wat Greer had been in the custody of the Bedford County Sheriff's office since the night of Detective Everson's murder on the 10th. After their incarceration, detectives interrogated the brothers about the murder of the railroad agent. Wat Greer denied any involvement in the events aboard the train. He did, however, indict his half-brother as the perpetrator. On the other hand, Dave Neal remained silent and sullen. He did say he witnessed the events but admitted to nothing that would implicate him in the facilitation of the murder.

Neither of the brothers was a novice when interacting with law enforcement officers. Both had very long arrest records dating back well into their youth.

A look at both men's arrest records would show a sordid and violent past. Both were charged with assault and battery on at least two occasions in the year before the murder. On November 24, 1910, Greer had gotten into a fight with another man in Chattanooga. A knife was pulled, and James Alexander, the other participant in the altercation, was cut, starting under his right ear and continuing around the back of the neck and almost to the mouth on the left side. The cut was so severe that it had taken numerous stitches to close it. When brought before a judge in Chattanooga City Court, Greer told the judge the cut had been inflicted when the two were "fooling around," and that he did it "for fun."

Tensions were running high in Shelbyville, with three murderers being held in the Bedford County Jail.

Rumors of an uprising and lynching were running rampant and had been since at least two days after the arrest of Neal and Greer. Sheriff Williams had wanted to move along the proceedings of binding over the two men. Shortly after the arrests, Sheriff Williams had been visited by a group of men from Shelbyville and others from out of the county who had insisted that Williams call a particular trial for the accused. In their words, they wanted swift justice for the two Negroes, and if it did not transpire quickly, they were going to enforce their justice not only on Neal and Greer but on Marion Anderson as well. (Anderson was still in Bedford County, having not been returned to Nashville after his hearing on February 1st.)

Knowing that this matter was almost coming to a boil, there had been a hasty meeting between the sheriff and the prosecutors. At one point, the conversation turned to alternatives, such as moving the preliminary hearing to one of the surrounding towns, such as Bell Buckle. Moving the hearing from Shelbyville surely would have calmed the tension building over the incarceration. Still, Williams vetoed the idea, citing security concerns about protecting the accused while moving them to a different location.

Now that the third suspect in Everson's killing, Charles Bomar, who had just been arrested in Chattanooga, was in the clutches of the sheriff, Williams and the county district attorney concluded that they had in custody everyone involved in the murder of the detective. With all three in custody, they felt comfortable moving forward with the prosecution of the accused murderers.

A preliminary hearing was set for 12:45 p.m. the following Monday in the second-story circuit courtroom of the historic Bedford

County Courthouse. Justice of the Peace John P. Brantley presided over the hearing.

The county's Attorney General, Thomas N. Greer, was the prosecutor assigned to try the case. Though he shared the same surname as the defendant, Charles Greer, they were no relation. Greer was also the same attorney who had been the prosecutor in the Marion Anderson preliminary hearing on February 1st.

General Greer had political aspirations, and prosecuting three Black men for the murder of a White policeman would generate just the kind of newspaper headlines he needed to launch a run for the office of governor of the state of Tennessee.

Having no money, the three defendants turned to the office of the Public Defender for representation. Their defense attorney would be the public defender, N.H. Crowell.

Monday, February 19, 1912, 1:00 p.m., Bedford County Courthouse

The Bedford County jail was located two blocks from the courthouse; the area between the two buildings was the perfect place for anyone with sinister motives to attack the prisoners and forcibly take them from the protection of the sheriff and his men. This point was not lost on Sheriff Williams. Williams was taking no chances that the rumored lynching would take place while Neal, Greer, and Bomar were in his custody. Since their arrests, Williams had called in extra deputies to protect the jail and its prisoners. On this, the day of the trial, a detail of six deputies was assigned to accompany and surround the three men as they walked between the two facilities.

Williams and his men had no idea of what lay ahead. About an hour before the sheriff and his deputies had wrangled the three defendants from their small cells in the Bedford County jail, a group of men, fellow NC&St.L employees of Detective Everson had boarded a train in Nashville heading for Shelbyville. For days, the accounts of the brutal killing of Detective Everson had played out detail by detail in the *Nashville Tennessean* and the *Nashville American* newspapers. A railroad detective was dead; the culprits were in custody in the jail in Shelbyville. One hundred miles away in Nashville, a group of angry men was formulating the idea that it was their responsibility to administer justice. Before the day was out, events in Shelbyville would take a deadly turn.

Greer, Neal, and Bomar took their places at the defense table. Greer and Neal wore faded black and white "zebra" pants and shirts. Bomar wore a striped top but was still wearing the pair of work jeans, the same ones he had been wearing the night he was taken into custody in Chattanooga by city police. In the jeans pocket was a folded-over pair of thick leather work gloves. Charles Bomar did not know it then, but those gloves would become the most critical items of clothing he had ever worn.

All three defendants were shackled together at the wrist. Under normal circumstances, the men would have also been manacled together at the ankles with leg irons to help prevent an attempted escape. For some reason, that procedure had not been followed on this day.

On Neal's head was a large, somewhat soiled bandage. No stranger to brushes with the law, he had previously been shot in the hand and the foot, and during a confrontation with a Shelbyville policeman only a few months before, he had been shot through the forehead. That bullet entered the front of Neal's head, passed through the left side of his head, and exited at the base of his skull. The bullet had somehow miraculously missed his brain and his spine. It had, however, made a substantial cavernous hole where his left eye had been. The dirty bandage, though ugly to see, at least covered the gaping black and purple wound.

A few minutes before the proceedings started, the three defendants could be seen conversing with their attorney, N.H. Crowell. Attorney Crowell told the three what would happen in the next few hours. He told them this was not a trial but simply a hearing of facts and a bond hearing to determine bail. It can be assured that he said to them that there was no chance that any bail would be set for three Negro defendants in a capital murder case of a policeman.

Justice Brantley gaveled the hearing to order as the large wall clock in the courtroom chimed out the one o'clock hour. The courtroom was filled past capacity; an official count was not taken, but estimates were that at least 250 people were packed into a room with a capacity of only 175. Spectators were standing around the outer walls of the courtroom, in some cases two feet deep.

After some opening remarks by Justice Brantley, Thomas N. Greer called the first four witnesses for the prosecution.

All witnesses, Jim Smalling, Tom Watson, Jim Johnson, and Sam Hatcher, were aboard the Jim Crow car that evening. Prosecutor Greer intended to weave a transparent tapestry of what had happened on the train the evening of the 10th. All four witnesses said that Wat Greer had been the person who had wrestled the gun away from the detective (a fact disputed in the statement of Greer after his arrest) and that it had been he who was the primary instigator of the actions that resulted in the death of Detective Everson.

Tom Watson went on to say that he was acquainted with the defendant, Dave Neal, and it did not surprise him that with Neal's hot temper, the situation between the defendant and the victim had gotten entirely out of hand.

The defense attorney called no witnesses and made no statements in his client's favor.

Justice Brantley found enough evidence of guilt to bind the three men over for trial and set a trial date for the April term of the circuit court. At this point, Defense attorney Crowell asked Justice Brantley if he might set bail for the defendants. That request was denied.

2:00 p.m., Bedford County Courthouse

And that was it. It had taken just over an hour. The hearing had gone smoothly, with no outbursts on anyone's part. The sheriff's deputies stood the defendants up, attached a set of chains to their wrists, and then shackled the three men together. The next move was getting the three men back safely to the jail two blocks from the courthouse.

What had not been noticed was that the courtroom had filled to overcapacity. Several persons in the crowded courtroom audience had been Detective Everson's friends and co-workers. Unknown to Sheriff Williams was the fact that the noon accommodation train to Shelbyville had brought as many as 20 men from Nashville, Chattanooga, and other areas whose sole purpose was to make sure that the men charged with the murder of the NC&St.L policeman would pay for the crime with their own lives.

As the proceedings started, these men had entered the courtroom quietly and without fanfare or commotion. Likewise, when Justice Brantley gaveled the hearing complete, they exited the room without tipping their hand about what was about to happen. The men left the room but then gathered along the balcony and the staircase leading down to the first floor of the building. In reality, they were setting a trap for the sheriff, and it was about to be sprung as the deputies and the defendants exited the courtroom.

The defendants, surrounded by a covey of about 20 deputies, exited the courtroom's double doors. Immediately, the crowd began to grow in its enmity. Seeing an opportunity, someone in the crowd yelled, "Let's get them!" A man at the top of the stairs drew a "blackjack" (a short, leather-covered, lead-filled club with a flexible handle) similar to the ones carried by peace officers. Suddenly, Wat Greer was stuck just behind the left ear by the weapon. The blow stunned him almost to senselessness. Several hands and arms reached for prisoner Bomar from the opposite side of the railings. A blast from a fist struck him in the back of his head. Several of the men then attempted to snatch Bomar away from the protection of the 40 to 45 deputies, who were now trying almost in vain to fight off the mob and, at the same time, hustle their wards down the stairs and to the safety of a nearby office.

Seeing that Bomar was about to be dragged from the control of the deputies, Sheriff Williams grabbed one of the assailants and threw him about five feet back into the crowd. This action incited the mob even more. The crowd rushed forward, trying to make yet another attempt at the prisoners and, this time, at the sheriff himself.

At this point, the situation was becoming most harrowing. As the deputies and the prisoners moved farther down the steps toward the first floor, the multitude of angry men separated the sheriff from his wards.

To escape what he was sure was his impending death, Bomar leaped over the staircase railing, but because he was still chained at the wrist to Wat Greer, Bomar became nothing more than a marionette attached by only one string. He began kicking his legs and whirling like a fish flailing on a fishhook.

Seeing the merciless condition now afflicting Bomar, some of the enraged group near the bottom of the steps grabbed at his legs in an attempt to pull him down to a place at which they might attack him again.

To this point, the sheriff had been carrying a long hickory stick. While some of the mob held him, one individual wrestled the stick from Sheriff Williams's grasp. With the stick in hand, a man jumped over the railing and began to use it on the now helplessly dangling Bomar.

Suddenly, everything stopped, if only for a moment. A shot from a pistol rang out. A bullet from the gun found its mark. Wat Greer sank to the risers, blood oozing from a wound on the left side of his head. He was dead before he hit the floor. With his collapse, Dave Neal and two sheriff's deputies also went down. On the other side of the stairs, the dangling weight of the half-conscious Charles Bomar pulled the mass of deputies and handcuffed men farther down the staircase until everyone was now just above the first-floor landing.

Sheriff Williams was finally able to break loose from the men who had been restraining him and bounded down the steps toward the mass of twisted bodies.

As he reached the bottom rung of the steps, Williams saw a second pistol rise to a firing position. The weapon was brought to the side of Charles Bomar's face, and just as the trigger was about to be pulled, the sheriff struck the pistol with a massive kick from the boot on his left foot.

Recoiling after the kick, the assailant returned the pistol to a firing position, but this time, it was pointed directly at the sheriff. Had it not been for the prompt actions of Deputy Bill "Wauhatchie" Frye, who dove at the man, knocking the pistol away, Sheriff Williams would have been shot as well.

Still struggling to get the men off the stairs, a hand-to-hand fight broke out between the officers and the crowd. For a few moments, this fight was a true life-or-death struggle, with the participants, including the prisoners, receiving cuts, abrasions, and blows as clubs, pistols, and fists flew from every direction. Somehow, in the middle of the melee, Deputies Bob Spenser and Henry Davis reached down and unlocked the manacles that bound Wat Greer to Bomar. Loosened from the shackles that bound him to the other two, Greer's body rolled down the last four risers and came to rest lifelessly on the first-floor tiles. Bomar fell atop the body of the fatally wounded man. Having already accosted Bomar with the hickory stick once, the assailant again raised the weapon above his shoulders, then struck Bomar with such force it broke the rod, splintering it into pieces.

2:05 p.m., Bedford County Courthouse

After the death of Greer, deputies aggressively fought to regain control of the violent conflict and dragged Bomar and Neal off the stairs and toward a first-floor office on the south side of the courthouse. For a few moments, the fisticuffs had decelerated, allowing the deputies to shuffle the two remaining prisoners toward safety. But within moments, the rear guard of the sheriff's men was attacked again. Caught in the middle of the scrimmage, Bomar and Neal were knocked to the ground. Pummeled about the head and body, the men were battered almost to insensibility. Deputy Bob Vanatta was able to retrieve the body of Wat Greer, dragging him along the floor. At the same time, Williams and the remaining deputies retreated and shielded the barely conscious Bomar and Neal. Finally, the group was able to drag Greer's body and the limp torsos of Neal and Bomar to the relative safety of the sheriff's office. The deputies unhandcuffed the two prisoners. Leaving the wounded and terrified men alone in the office, the deputies were able to slam shut a door between Neal and Bomar, and the mob attempting to kill them.

Sheriff Williams ordered the office doors and windows barricaded. A massive guard contingency was strategically placed in the hallway and the exterior stairway to protect Neal and Bomar from additional harm.

Since the senseless murder of Detective Everson and the earlier murders of Officers Purdy and Henry by Marion Anderson, Sheriff Williams had been very much aware that the threat of lynching of the four men he had in custody was a high probability.

In trying to protect his prisoner and simultaneously quell some of the anger exhibited by the people of Bedford County, just after the murder of the two policemen, he had transported Marion Anderson out of Shelbyville and to the protection of the county jail in Nashville. He had not afforded the three Negroes the same security as he had done with the White defendant. This was not a matter of race but had to do more with economics. The costs of housing Anderson in Nashville and having to transport him back and forth to the capital city for hearings and his eventual trials were already starting to mount up, and county officials would not authorize the expense of housing the other three men in another county. Besides, as had happened, today's incident occurred when the three were in the county for a hearing. Housing them in another facility would not have changed that matter. One thing was assured: the murder of a second policeman in the county had tipped the scales, a lynching had occurred, the sheriff had haunting trouble before him ... and it was not over.

With Wat Greer's homicide and his two co-defendants' escape from death by the slimmest of margins, the sheriff realized the situation was exceedingly out of control. Hiring the additional special deputies had not prevented what had just happened on the staircase. If he were to maintain the peace, he would need extra manpower—and a lot of it.

Around 3:00 p.m., the situation at the courthouse had stabilized, and the danger had, if not passed, been less contentious. Leaving his office in the hands of his men, Williams and one of his deputies slipped out one of the side doors of his office in the courthouse and made their way to the law office of W.H. Crowell to make a phone call. Crowell's office on the ground floor of the Dixie Hotel at Main and Martin Streets contained one of only three telephones in the city at the time, and Williams needed the phone to make a long-distance call to Nashville. The sheriff contacted the Bell System telephone operator and asked to be put through to the office of Tennessee Governor Ben W. Hooper in the state capitol. Hooper had anticipated the call, as he had been monitoring the situation in Shelbyville ever since he had been informed of the arrests of the three Black men.

In a conversation with the sheriff a few days before the trial, the governor had already offered troops from the Tennessee State Militia to reinforce the Bedford County force. Williams had assured the governor that he could handle any uprisings and had turned down the offer. That afternoon, the situation had dramatically changed.

The sheriff informed Governor Hooper of what had transpired inside the courthouse. The sheriff told the governor that, at least for the moment, he had the situation under control, but he feared an escalation of violence could happen at any moment. Hooper told the sheriff that he thought it best to muster a Tennessee State Guard company and have them board the first available train to Shelbyville. Then, the call from Shelbyville ended. The governor called the state militia's office, and troops were ordered to arm.

3:45 p.m., On the Streets of Shelbyville

Several of the lynch mob had dispersed outside the courthouse and were wandering the streets of the city. After calling the governor,

Sheriff Williams and his deputy tried to return to his office in the courthouse to check on Neal and Bomar's welfare. A half block from the attorney's office, all of a sudden, the two found themselves surrounded by a group of men—with guns drawn. The men had surrounded them so quickly ... and were holding them at gunpoint, preventing the sheriff and his deputy from returning to check on the welfare of the two remaining prisoners.

After neutralizing the sheriff, in what can only be assumed was a coordinated measure, another set of men entered the south entrance of the courthouse and proceeded toward the sheriff's office. With the arrival of this second group of rioters, the sound of breaking glass resonated through the south side of the building. The butt of a gun was used to break the glass in the door of the sheriff's main floor office. Several men climbed through the newly created opening and overpowered deputies Bob Vanatta, Douglas Dye, Harry McAdams, Horace Watkins, John Moore, and M. Taylor, who, up to this point, had heroically risked their lives to protect Neal and Bomar. One of the men in the mob (later described as a "low man with a black mustache"), pistol in hand, made his way to the center of the room, where he found Neal lying in a half fetal position. Pointing the pistol at Neal's head, he coolly discharged the weapon. The bullet entered the helpless man's head on his left side just behind the ear. At the repeat of the firearm, Neal's body jerked as the projectile entered, then fell into a lifeless pose.

Only a few feet away, Charles Dane Bomar witnessed the assassin shoot and murder David Neal. The semi-conscious Bomar leaped to his feet and ran for the protection of a large wooden desk in the corner of the room. The assassin turned the revolver in his hand toward the fleeing man and fired. For whatever reason, the man wielding the gun did not aim for Bomar's head. The round struck the prisoner in the upper part of his right leg. Bomar instinctively dropped to the floor behind the desk and feigned death. Thinking that he had accomplished his mission of killing both men, the gunman turned away, climbed over the shards of broken glass in the door, and exited into the hallway. Closely following the gunman, the rest of the men who had broken into the office withdrew back into the hallway and then hurried into the courtyard outside of the building and toward the train depot three blocks away.

Now, no longer at the point of a gun, the deputies in the office immediately turned to check the status of Neal and Bomar. Dave Neal was in critical condition, as he had sustained a severe wound to his head. He was bleeding out into a large pool of blood on the floor. Dane Bomar, on the other hand, had been lucky. He had been shot, but fortuitously, the bullet had been slowed and then stopped entirely by a pair of heavy buckskin work gloves Bomar had doubled over and stuck in the right front pocket of his pants.

Bomar was frightened almost to hysterics, considering what he had just undergone. Still, he was alive, and other than the severe head wounds inflicted upon him during the first attempt on the prisoners' lives, he was relatively unhurt.

At the same time the party of lynchers had been exiting the courthouse, some of the sheriff's deputies realized that the sheriff and some of the other deputies were being held at gunpoint by members of the mob. Immediately, they rushed to their aid. When the men in the mob saw the law officers coming to the rescue of their hostages, they lowered their weapons and retreated to join the mass of men moving to the east of the square.

At least one witness reported that after the assassin had broken through the glass in the door of the sheriff's office and had attempted to lynch the prisoners, he walked out of the courthouse and entered a local bar where he had a drink. The assassin then walked to the NC&St.L depot and boarded the 4:20 p.m. accommodation train that would take him back to Wartrace. Alighting on the station platform in Wartrace, he awaited the northbound No.6 that would take him back toward Nashville. The man was not alone in his departure from the havoc that day. Along with him were the other mob members (estimated to have been more than 70 men) who had descended on Shelbyville on the noon train. Likewise, they purchased a return fare, and they, too, departed on the 4:20 p.m. train. These men changed trains in Wartrace, and it was later reported that when the Nashville-bound train reached Bell Buckle, 43 of the passengers exited the train at that location.

Back in Nashville, Governor Hooper did everything he could to halt any additional outbreaks in Shelbyville. Within 30 minutes of Sheriff Williams's initial call, Hooper, as commander-in-chief of the Tennessee Guard, instructed guard officers to muster men together as soon as possible to react to the violence. He also placed a call to the NC&St.L Railway, asking them to assemble a special train to ferry the troops from Union Station in Nashville to Shelbyville.

C.R. Rogan, a captain with the guard, was responsible for mobilizing the troops. He, along with Captain J.C. Boyle, Major John H. Samuel, and Lieutenant Fitzhugh, hastily raised a company of about 50 men from various local guard companies.

At about the same time the guardsmen were mustering at Union Station and were about to board the train, the governor received a second phone call. Sheriff Williams called to report that the men who formed the lynch mob had boarded the outbound local train and had already left town. The sheriff perceived the threat to have been quashed, and the services of the military units would no longer be required.

With this news, Hooper realized the troops would not be needed in Bedford County. He sent word to Captains Rogan and Boyle to position men at Nashville's Union Station to intercept the No.6 train as it came in from Wartrace. It had been reported that some of the mob's leaders were probably men from Nashville. Governor Hooper devised a plan to arrest these leaders when they arrived aboard the inbound train. But who were the troops supposed to look for? The governor called Shelbyville to obtain a description of the mob leaders. The call did not reach Sheriff Williams, and it was soon learned that no attempt had been made to identify those who had boarded the Shelbyville accommodation train as it departed back to Wartrace.

Realizing that no arrests could be made without proper identification of the suspects, Governor Hooper then turned to an alternative of offering a reward of $500 each for the capture and conviction of any of the mob members, the total of the rewards to be at most $5,000. A bulletin was sent to the Nashville Police stating that the reward was in effect. It was hoped the reward would garner the policemen's interest in ascertaining the mob leaders' identities.

The guardsmen were ordered to stand down and were told to return to their previous activities. In anticipation that trouble might again rear its head in Shelbyville, Captain Boyle and several guardsmen, instead of returning to their homes, made their way to the armory on Union Street, where they would spend the night. By staying in town, they would be available for a quick callout if the need arose.

The Bedford County-appointed physician, Doctor F.P. Ready, was quickly summoned to attend to the two wounded prisoners at the courthouse. The doctor determined that Neal was in grave condition and that his prognosis was guarded. It seemed barely possible that he might recover from this latest attempt on his life. Neal's head was severely swollen from the beating he had received when struck with the clubs and from the damage done by the bullet. The wound to Bomar's head was bandaged, although he had been attacked

"Big Jim" Williams, wife, and four of his five children. ca. 1907.
Photo credit, Norm Williams

"The Rock" Bedford County Jail (built 1867).
Photo credit, Norm Williams.

Passenger Train ca. 1912.   Photo Credit, NC&St.L Ry.

Marion Eldridge Anderson, 1912. Photo Credit, Bedford County, Tennessee Archives

Four Shelbyville Policemen, Front L to R: Officer Redin G. Purdy, Officer Charles Henry. One of the two men in the back row is presumed to be Officer Hiram H. Rittenberry. Photo credit, Judy Phillips.

Photo of Marion Anderson Trial. April 16, 1912. At the center of the photo is Sheriff James Williams. At the center of the photograph, L to R, the defense attorney, Marion Anderson, and the prosecutor are seated at the table. Directly below the defendant, the white-haired man (not facing the camera) is Judge John E. Richardson. The jury members are at the lower part of the photograph, and Mrs. Tennie Anderson is hiding from the camera behind the chair.   Photo credit, Norm Williams.

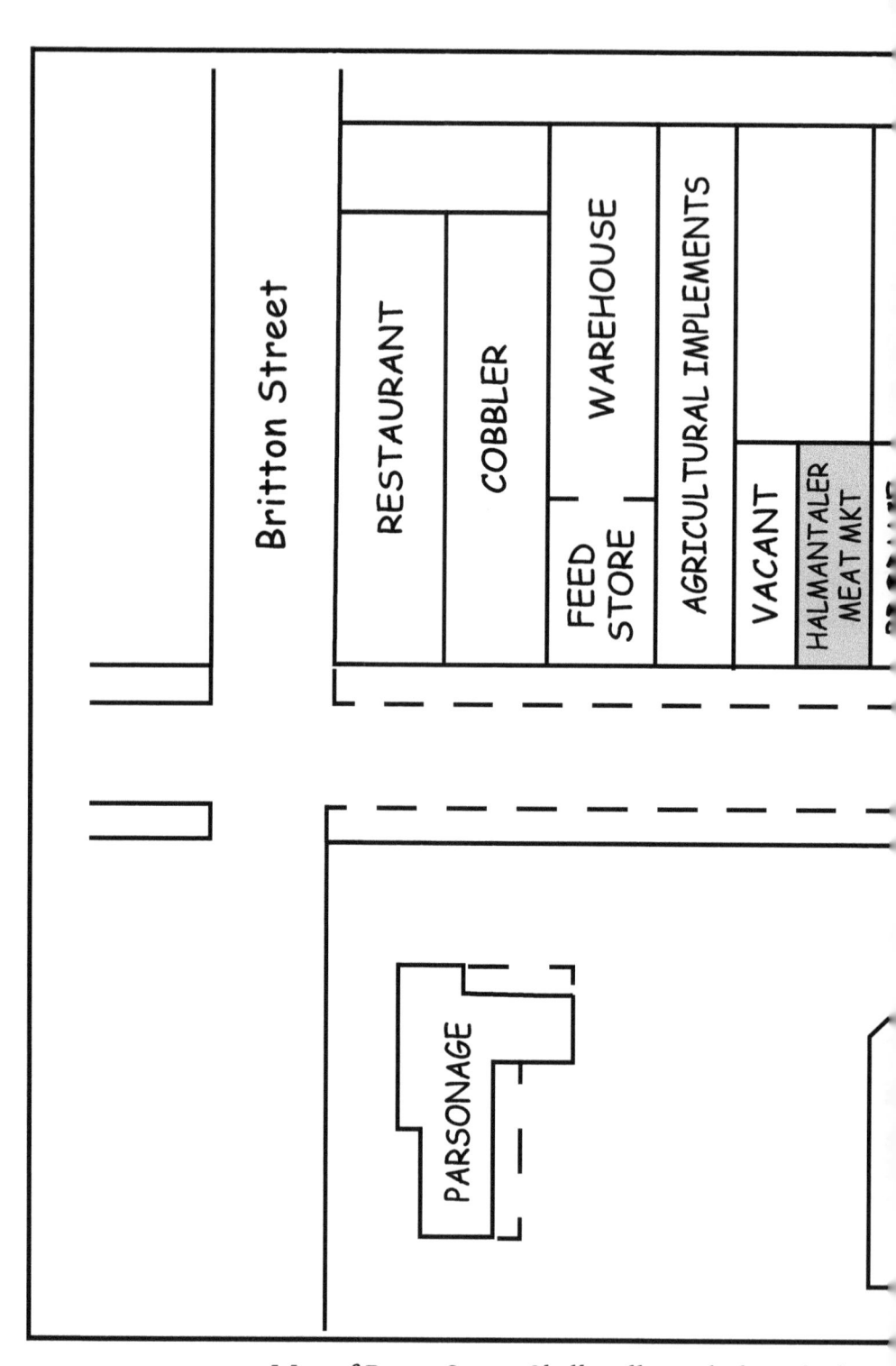

Map of Depot Street, Shelbyville, including the locat

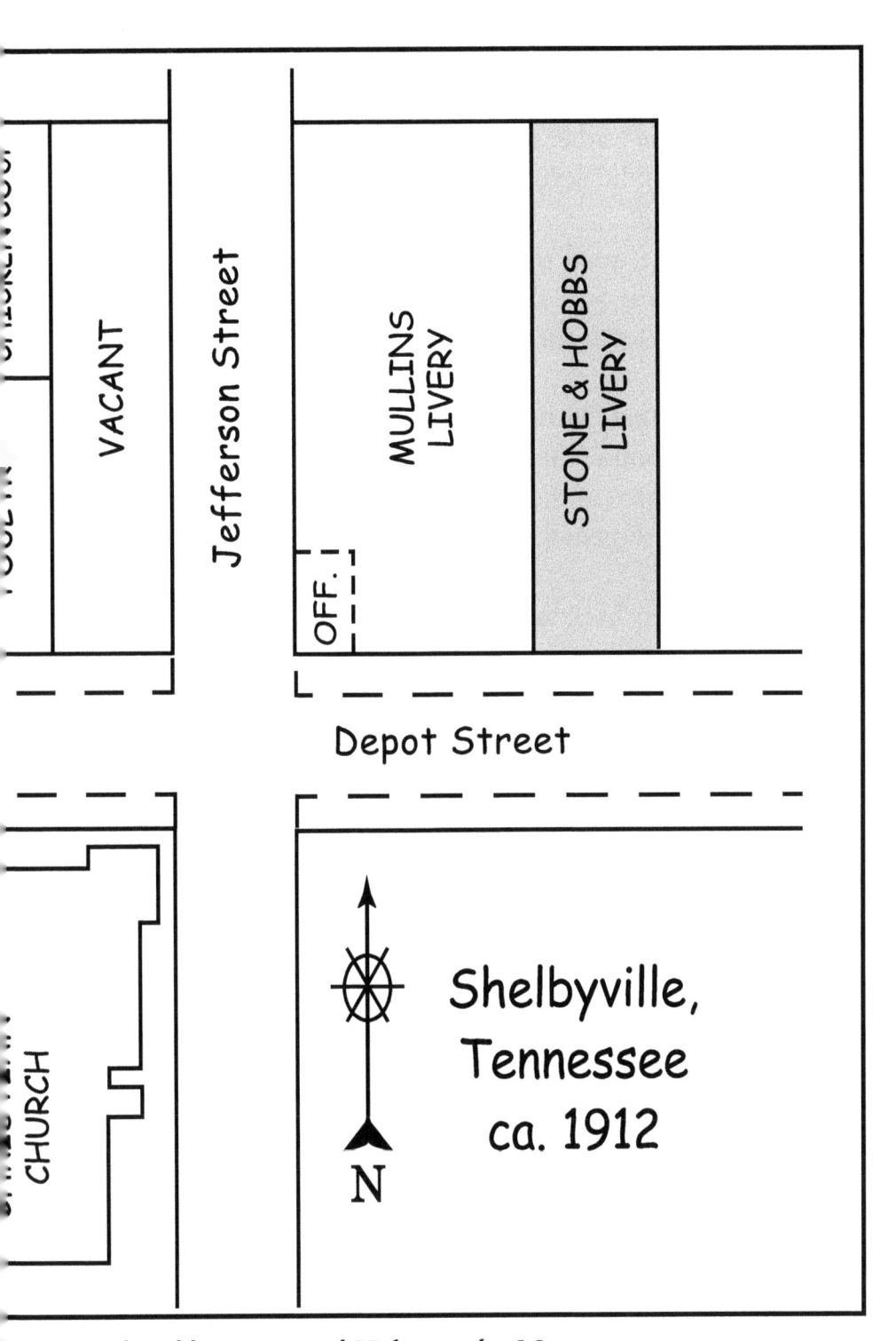

Stone and Hobbs Livery and Halmantaler Meats.

numerous times with fists and a heavy wood stick had been broken in half with an assault on him, it appeared that he had not sustained broken bones. The leather gloves in his pants pocket had stopped the bullet. A day later, he developed a tremendous bruise on his thigh.

After the doctor treated the wounds bandages were applied under heavy guard, Neal and Bomar, were transported by makeshift ambulance back down the hill to the jail.

At the same time that Doctor Ready was attending to the two assaulted men at the courthouse, the body of Wat Greer lay on the embalmer's table in the basement of the Jackson and Sons funeral home, the only "Colored" establishment for such purposes in Shelbyville.

With the prisoners back safely in jail and those who had descended upon the town with nefarious intent again out of the city, Sheriff Williams felt again that the immediate danger had passed. He returned to Attorney W.H. Crowell's office to phone the governor again and ask for the stand-down order.

And that was it. As quickly as the mob had arrived in the city, they had departed with the same expediency. The citizens of Shelbyville were quick to point out that even though the emotions of the people of the county had flared to red hot, the actions of this day had not been carried out by anyone from Shelbyville or Bedford County. This, of course, would directly contradict the assumption by the sheriff that it had been men of the county who had participated in the actions of the day. The fact that 43 men had exited the afternoon train in Bell Buckle after the lynch mob departed Shelbyville would undoubtedly confirm the sheriff's belief.

Nonetheless, the citizens would point out that if it had been some men from Bedford County who had been in the crowd, they had not directly participated in the murder. Those with blood on their hands, the real villains, had been outside agitators, presumably from Nashville and possibly Chattanooga, who had descended on the county seat like a swarm of locusts. Rumor had it that the mob leaders had been railroad employees who had left their jobs on an avenging mission for one of their own.

It is plausible that the men of Bedford County had not murdered anyone. Sheriff Williams, in a report, stated that in his estimate, there had been about 50 men who actively took part in the lynching. These 50 had been encouraged by a group of 500 or so, and as many as 1,500 others did no more than watch what had happened.

At 5:00 p.m. that afternoon, Judge W.E. Grant convened a coroner's inquiry to determine who had been responsible for the murder of Wat Greer and the attempted murder of Neal and Bomar. Doctor Ready, the same physician who had treated Neal and Bomar's wounds earlier in the day, was the primary witness at the hearing. Ready said that it was his professional opinion that there was about an equal chance that Dave Neal would pull through or that he would not live to see the morning light. After a short deliberation, it was determined that the death of Greer had been at the hands of "a person or persons unknown," a term that was used too many times when it came to the lynching of a Black man, but was also a term well known in cases like this. The matter was closed pending any additional information becoming known.

As it turned out, Doctor Ready's assessment that Dave Neal would either recover entirely or die before the following day was right and wrong. Dave Neal split the difference and, as reported in the *Shelbyville Gazette,* died of his injuries on March 11. This grizzly individual, shot in the head for a second time, had been fatally wounded.

Peace prevailed in Shelbyville on the evening of February 19th, but Sheriff Williams anticipated he might have to deal with additional trouble. He and about 25 of his men stationed themselves in and around the jail to protect Neal and Bomar and maintain the peace. Fortunately, no more trouble was created, and everyone had a peaceful night.

Governor Hooper's offer of $500 for the arrest and conviction of a mob participant was never claimed. Only one arrest was made. On April 4, 1912, Jesse Phillips, a prominent farmer formerly from the Richmond community in Bedford County, was arrested near his Baucom, Coffee County residence. Three Bedford County deputies took him into custody after a Circuit Court Grand Jury handed down an indictment on the charge of his participation in the mobbing and murder of Neal and Greer and injuring Dane Bomar. Five days later, Phillips had made a bond in the case.

An article in the *Chattanooga Times* speculated that this arrest would be the first of several to follow. They were wrong. No other person was arrested. In August, Phillips was tried in Shelbyville on the charge of second-degree murder. He was acquitted of all charges because of a lack of evidence.

Chapter Six

The First Trial of Marion Anderson

Saturday, April 13, 1912, Shelbyville, Tennessee: Jury Selection

On Saturday, April 13th, the principals in the long-awaited trial of Marion Anderson assembled in the same courtroom that had been the site of the preliminary hearing for the three suspects in the Everson murder trial. Present were the defendant, his defense attorney Thomas R. Myers and his son, attorney Paul R. Myers, and an associate, attorney J.D. Murphree.

Attorney General Walter S. Faulkner and his assistants, General Ernest Shepard and Attorney General Thomas N. Greer (General Greer had been the lead prosecutor in the murder case of Officer Everson), were present for the prosecution.

Rutherford County Circuit Court Judge John E. Richardson was brought in to preside over this case. Richardson had a reputation for being strict but fair.

In his opening statements, Judge Richardson informed all present in the courtroom that the case before them was only for the murder of Officer R.G. Purdy, one of the two policemen slain on the night of October 31, 1911. The other case, the murder of Officer Henry, would be tried at a later date.

Judge Richardson and the prosecutor Attorney General Faulkner were anxious to avoid another delay in getting this trial underway. Richardson was far away from his home three counties away. For Faulkner, this trial had been postponed several times, and costs were skyrocketing for the county. With each postponement, there was the expense of transporting the defendant between Nashville and Shelbyville, and the county had to provide extra security details to guard the prisoner and the courthouse at each appearance.

As it had been for the preliminary hearing, security for the start of the trial was extraordinarily heavy. An additional 25 officers were deputized to fortify the personnel needed to maintain the peace.

This morning, the judge demanded the courtroom remain vacant apart from those who were essential for jury selection. Six deputies were assigned to the bottom of the stairs on the courthouse's first floor. Each of the over 650 potential veniremen was searched before proceeding up the stairs. An additional four deputies were assigned to the entrance of the courtroom. There was no way Sheriff Williams was going to allow a repeat of the shameful violence that had happened on February 19th when a mob overpowered his men and murdered two of the three defendants in the Everson murder case.

By 9:00 a.m., all the potential jurors and several potential witnesses were present in the courtroom. The defendant was brought into the courtroom at 9:15, escorted by ten deputies.

Upon entering, Anderson, dressed in a clean but somewhat tattered suit, looked tired and noticeably pale. His long confinement in jail was beginning to wear on him both physically and emotionally. But a few minutes later, his attitude seemed to improve when he caught sight of his wife, several friends, and other supporters entering the rear of the courtroom.

Tennie waved and then flashed what seemed to be an adoring smile at the defendant before taking her place in the gallery directly behind the table at which her husband was sitting. The courtroom gallery seemed to be divided, with Mrs. Anderson and the friends of the defendant on one side and the family and those in support of the slain police officers on the other.

Moments later, Judge Richardson entered the room and gaveled the proceedings into session. After a few opening statements by the judge, he asked if the prosecution and the defense were ready to proceed with jury selection.

An hour's recess was taken at 12:30 p.m. for lunch. When the court reconvened, the same rigorous security was exercised as had been in place during the forenoon session. Officers again were placed at the foot of the stairs. Just as with the morning session, everyone wishing to ascend the steps to the courtroom was thoroughly searched before they could pass.

Another short adjournment was taken. When the court reconvened just after 3:00 p.m., jury selection began. By day's end, 12 jurors, S.W. Lentz, John Parsons, J.C. Barrett, Joe Faulk, W.S. Waldrin, C. Stallings, E.A. Beasley, John Parsons, J.C. Barnett, Grace Shearin, Horace Anderson (no relation to the defendant), W.A.J. Poplin, and two alternates had been selected, seated, and were ready to serve. Another juror, E. Woodfin, picked initially to serve, was dismissed when it was learned that he was a distant relative of one of the slain police officers.

With the jury in place, Judge Richardson asked if the attorneys were ready to proceed.

General Faulkner rose and announced that the prosecution was ready to proceed with the trial. Immediately, attorney Thomas Myers stood and asked for a continuance. Myers told the judge there were eight witnesses important to the defense who were not present, but that they could be located in short order. Judge Richardson was a bit perturbed by Myers's request for a continuance. The judge admonished him for not having the witnesses at hand but granted the request.

Upon reconvening the court, attorney Myers read the statements of several witnesses who, he said, would give his client an alibi on the night of the shooting. Three of those statements contended that the defendant was not even in Shelbyville at the time of the murders and that he had left town around 8:30 p.m., almost an hour before the shots rang out. Others said that Anderson had left town to visit relatives in Coffee County.

Myers was attempting to get a summary judgment from the court, thus circumventing the need for a trial. Judge Richardson was having none of it.

Juror selection and preliminary matters from the attorneys took up most of the day this Saturday. Judge Richardson told everyone involved that opening statements would commence the following Monday. All those involved were instructed to report back to the courthouse on Monday, and the proceeding was gaveled to a close for the day.

As a large contingent of local citizens watched, Marion Anderson was returned to the Shelbyville jail by a massive armada of sheriff's deputies. Over 40 deputies patrolled the streets of Shelbyville, and more would be stationed inside the courthouse. The trial was set to start at 9:00 a.m. on Monday, April 15th.

Monday, April 15, 1912, Day One of the Trial

On Monday, promptly at 8:30 a.m., the defendant, surrounded by eight of Sheriff Williams's deputies, departed the jail and was escorted up the hill to the courthouse. Security inside the courthouse was robust, with three officers stationed at the foot of the stairs leading up to the courtroom on the second floor. The deputies vigorously scrutinized every person who was trying to gain access to the courtroom. They were only allowed to pass after a search for weapons, and if, in the deputies' opinion, they did not exhibit any hostility toward the defendant,

The trial included a plethora of attorneys for the defense and for the State as well. Defending Marion Anderson was Thomas P. Myers, his son (a friend of the defendant), Paul B. Myers, and lead attorney J.P. Murphree. Attorneys for the prosecution were General W.S. Faulkner and Assistant District Attorney Thomas, who tried the case for the State of Tennessee, N. Greer (who had tried the three Black defendants in the Everson murder), E.C. Parker, Judge A. Shepard, and General E. Caldwell.

There was much tension in the gallery of the courtroom. Sitting directly behind the prosecution's table were the families of both Officer Purdy and Officer Henry. Even though this was a trial for the murder of Officer Purdy only, members of the Henry family were there to give moral support to the Purdy family. Mrs. Laura Purdy, dressed in deep mourning clothing, was accompanied by her two married daughters. When the defendant was ushered into the courtroom, Belle Purdy buried her face into her hands and began to sob uncontrollably.

On the other side of the courtroom, behind the defense attorney's table, sat a large contingent of Marion Anderson's friends and relatives. Others in the gallery later reported that tensions between the two factions were so thick they could have been cut with a knife.

In his opening statement, Attorney General Faulkner read to the all-male jury the indictment from the Bedford County grand jury charging Marion Anderson, a citizen of Shelbyville, with the brutal murder on the night of October 31, 1911, of two Shelbyville city policemen, R.G. Purdy and Charles Henry. As Judge Richardson had done earlier, he reiterated that the trial before them was only for finding guilt or innocence in the murder of Officer Purdy.

At that point, Judge Richardson asked the defendant to plead guilty or not guilty to the charges. Anderson and his attorney, Thomas Myers, stood, faced the judge, and answered in a clear and resounding voice, "Not guilty, Your Honor."

The first witnesses called by the State were F.P. Beardon, operator of the local funeral home, and Doctor T.R. Ray, to establish the cause of death of the policeman. Beardon stated that he examined the body of Officer Purdy and found that he had been shot twice, once in the left breast and once in the right arm, and that shot had passed through the officer's body and had exited just below the left armpit. On follow-up, Doctor Ray echoed the findings of the undertaker and stated that it was his opinion that the officer had succumbed to injuries from the gunshots.

Officer Purdy's uniform coat, still replete with dried blood stains, was given to Doctor Ray, who, upon exiting the witness stand, held the coat up before the jury. Pointing at the bullet holes in the coat, he illustrated the path each bullet had taken and the damage it had inflicted.

At the sight of the blood-stained coat, Mrs. Purdy again buried her face in her fan and began to sob just as she had done when first witnessing the defendant's presence in the courtroom.

The next witness for the State was the person everyone in the courtroom had been waiting to hear from. The State introduced S.M. Rayburn, who was the only person to be closely associated with Anderson on the night of the murder and who would testify that he had heard him confess to the killing.

From the witness stand, Rayburn proceeded to recount the events of the evening of October 31st. He told the jury that he had been uptown and returned to the livery a little after 8:00 p.m. to find his cousin, who he said was very drunk, and two other men removing the harness of a pale-yellow horse hitched to a buggy. He recounted that Anderson had to go to another livery to obtain a saddle when a proper one could not be found in the establishment where they worked.

Rayburn went on to say that at that point, one of the two men in the stable, Mr. Burris, attempted to talk the defendant into going upstairs to his residence to sleep off his intoxication.

For the next one and a half hours, Rayburn continued point by point, laying out in detail the events of the night of the murder. He stated that Marion refused to go upstairs at Mr. Burris's request. Instead, he continued to saddle the horse. After riding away, Anderson returned a short time later and hitched the horse's reins to the front door of the livery. Rayburn said he assumed Anderson had returned for the evening and asked if he could remove the saddle and care for the animal. Instead, Anderson walked away from the stable and headed west toward the courthouse square. Within minutes, shots were heard, and a short time later, Anderson returned to the livery almost out of breath with beads of sweat upon his brow. He had a pistol in his hand.

General Faulkner interrupted, saying, "Mr. Rayburn, let me stop you right there. I want the jury to understand clearly what you are about to testify. On the night of the 31st of October …" Faulkner wanted to ensure the witness's next statement would be clear and concise. He knew that the words from Rayburn's lips were essential for the prosecution; his entire case rode on the way the following testimony would be presented, and he did not want it to go awry.

Thomas Myers immediately jumped to his feet with an objection. "Your honor, my esteemed colleague is leading this witness."

"Sustained," said the judge.

"I'm sorry; I sometimes get ahead of myself," said Faulkner, turning back toward the witness. "Please continue."

Rayburn's answer would be the turning point in his testimony. Rayburn shifted slightly in the witness box, looking straight at his cousin, and said, "When he returned out of the darkness, he said, 'I got 'em both.'"

"And when did he say this?"

"As he made his way toward the yellow mare he had tied outside. Hearing the commotion and realizing that her husband had returned to the livery, Mrs. Anderson ran out to where he was about to ride away and screamed at him. He then heard Marion call back to her, 'I got 'em both.'"

Rayburn added that Mrs. Anderson shouted, "O Daddy, O Daddy, what made you do that?"

At this point, Anderson, following the testimony closely, became upset and began fidgeting in his chair. A loud murmur resounded through the courtroom as the audience responded to the witness's testimony. Several people jumped to their feet, and voices were raised. Order was restored only after Judge Richardson rapped his gavel loudly on his bench.

General Faulkner asked one more question, "Mr. Rayburn, after Mr. Anderson shouted out the words you just repeated here, did you see him leave, and if so, in what direction did he go?"

"He mounted the horse and rode toward the depot with the pistol still in his hand."

Faulkner closed, "No more questions of this witness, your honor."

It was now the defense's turn to do some damage control. Attorney Thomas Myers rose and walked toward the witness box. During cross-examination, he needed to impeach this witness by questioning him about his past life. Rayburn's testimony had been damning. It was Myers's job to lessen the impact of that testimony.

The opening question for the defense was, "Mr. Rayburn, isn't it true that Captain Allen of the sheriff's department took you to jail and charged you with murder?"

"Yes, I was taken in, but only to answer questions about Mr. Anderson's whereabouts." (This was only a half-truth. Rayburn had made threats against the police because he suspected they had been watching him, sure that Rayburn along with Anderson had been bootlegging whiskey out of the livery. With the death of the two policemen, detectives from the sheriff's office wanted to follow up on those threats.)

The witness answered that someone had, but he could not remember who. Additional questions along this line evoked only negative responses from the witness. He was unable to recall just what had happened after Anderson disappeared. Myers then asked, "Didn't you swear at the coroner's inquest that you and Mrs. Anderson were upstairs at the time of this occurrence and that you did not know anything about the actions of the defendant?"

Rayburn answered that he did not know. Myers remarked, "How can you remember what you testified to just a week later?" Myers had rattled the witness and had weakened his testimony concerning the actions of the defendant on the night of the murders.

The witness stated that he had been arrested and that everything confused him.

Nothing else was gained from this line of questioning.

Rayburn was dismissed, but Myers asked for the rule (the witness would remain under oath and available to be recalled if needed for further testimony) in case he might want to recall the witness later.

Walter Hickerson was the next witness introduced by the State. In his testimony, he related that his home was about two miles from Normandy and within two hundred yards of the Coffee/Bedford County line. After being asked several questions by Attorney Greer, Hickerson related that late on the night of October 31st, the defendant rode up to his house on a pale-yellow horse and asked for directions to Robert's Ridge.

Upon further questioning, Hickerson continued, "He then asked if it would be all right for him to spend the night. I agreed to let him stay. He took the horse to the barn and later came to the house, where we gave him something to eat."

"I noted that he was up around 4:00 a.m. on Wednesday, but then, strangely, he spent all day holding up in my corncrib. That afternoon, when I took him some supper out to the crib, he asked me to ride into Normandy and buy him some cartridges."

Greer asked, "And did you purchase the cartridges as he asked? Did you ask him why he needed them?"

"No, I never got into town, but he related that some policemen had roughed him up after he was arrested and that he had had some trouble with them," testified Hickerson.

He added, "He did not tell me that he killed two men but did say that he had gotten into some trouble in Shelbyville. I learned from my postal carrier that there was a posse of over 300 men covering the area looking for the fugitive."

"When Anderson left my place that night, he asked for some turpentine, saying that if such a large group of men were tracking him, they would indeed have bloodhounds, and the turpentine would throw the dogs off his trail. I noticed that Mr. Anderson used the turpentine I presented to dab it upon his shoes just before he left."

Hickerson concluded his testimony: "Upon leaving, Anderson asked me to take his yellow horse out to the road and let him loose, instead, I tied the horse to a tree just down the road from my home."

This completed the questioning by the State. The defense attorneys asked this witness no questions.

Following Walter Hickerson, the court heard from three more prosecution witnesses: H.H. Rittenberry, the policeman who had arrested Anderson before the murders that evening; J.E. Burris, who covered Anderson's bond after Officer Rittenberry and Officer Purdy had arrested him; and E.C. Halmantaler, in front of whose butcher shop the officers had been gunned down on Halloween night.

With the conclusion of the State's primary case, one thing was sure: the prosecution had made a convincing case that Marion Anderson had murdered the two Shelbyville police officers, and he had done it with forethought.[5]

The court then adjourned for the evening.

Tuesday, April 16, 1912, Day Two of the Trial

Since his apprehension on murder charges, Marion Anderson had been champing at the bit to appear in open court and relate his version of the events of the previous Halloween night. Anderson contended that he did not kill the police officers, but it would be brought out in court who did.

On April 16th, the second day of the trial, he got the chance he had been waiting for.

Some facts in the case were not in dispute. Anderson had to admit to those facts and work them into his alibi.

There was no doubt that Anderson had left Shelbyville the night of October 31st on horseback … check.

---

[5] The events in Shelbyville on the first day of the trial were vastly overshadowed by breaking news from the North Atlantic Ocean.

On the night of April 14th at around 23:40, ship's time, RMS Titanic struck an iceberg on her maiden voyage. The ship had set sail from Southampton, England, on the 10th of April. After stopping at Cherbourg, France, and Queensland, Ireland, the ship departed on a transatlantic voyage headed for the United States.

The ship's crew had received repeated warnings of sea ice and icebergs, but for the most part, they had dismissed the warnings. The ship struck an iceberg approximately 550 miles east of Newfoundland, ripping a hole along her starboard side. The collision slashed a 300-foot-long gash across the forepeak. The impact sliced a hole in three bulkhead compartments and two engine rooms. The damage was too extensive for the ship to remain afloat, and in a little over two and a half hours, it went down by the bow, broke in half, and sank, taking with it the 1500 persons still aboard.

Regulations in 1912 did not mandate ocean liners carry enough lifeboats for a complete abandonment at one time by every person on board. The ship was sailing under safety regulations that had originated nearly 20 years earlier. The Titanic was governed by regulations for any ship 10,000 tons and up. The Titanic weighed 46,000 tons, more than four times the weight the regulations were designed for. Officials maintained that ships had become much safer and revising the regulations was unnecessary. That regulation required Titanic to have only 16 lifeboats; Titanic had 20.

The prevailing thought was that the ship could serve as a gigantic lifeboat. No one could conceive of the chain of events that freezing April night. Nearly everyone

He stopped at the farm of Walter Hickerson, where he spent the night and most of the following day hiding ... check.

At some point, he did go to his father's house and the house of his attorney, Paul Myers ... check.

After agreeing on these facts, Anderson would have to be very creative about how the facts played out. His story differed from the other witnesses' accounts.

Marion Anderson and Mrs. Anderson entered the courtroom under heavy guard. He looked sallow and fatigued after the trying testimony on Monday afternoon. She, too, was showing signs that

---

believed that even a heavily damaged vessel would remain afloat for many hours before sinking. When the smaller liner Republic was involved in a collision in 1909, she remained afloat for more than 24 hours. All 742 passengers and crew were ferried to safety. That would allow plenty of time for the lifeboats to go back and forth several times, transporting passengers to nearby ships. It was assumed that in the case of an emergency, there would be other ships in the proximity of any damaged vessel that could come to its aid. This assumption seemed reasonable and was held on the night the Titanic encountered the iceberg. There were at least three ships near the damaged Titanic that night: the Californian, the Carpathia, and a mystery ship that has never been identified. Unfortunately, the wireless operator aboard the Californian had turned off his wireless only minutes before a distress signal from RMS Titanic went forth. The Carpathia acknowledged the signal but was about four hours sailing distance from a ship that sank in less than two and a half hours. The Carpathia did arrive at the site of the sinking, but by the time it arrived, there was nothing it could do other than to rescue the 700 or so passengers who had been lucky enough to reach one of the lifeboats. All others had either drowned or frozen to death in the 25-degree water. Why the unknown mystery ship did not respond to wireless signals or the sending up of distress flares is still unknown. This ship simply sailed away.

Unfortunately, the Titanic was not equipped with enough boats to evacuate all 2,225 passengers at once. Of that number, more than 1,500 were not rescued and perished in the accident. The loss of the "unsinkable" Titanic sent shock waves across Europe and the U.S.

A moment of silence was observed in the courtroom at the start of the proceedings on Tuesday morning.

the trial was taking its toll; her appearance was gaunt and pale. It was apparent that the strain she had endured over the last few months had been difficult.

Before the testimony on Monday, Anderson had been calm and almost apathetic in following witnesses' testimony. During the preliminary hearing, he was free with his answers to the questions and answered them without fear. This all changed after listening to the statements of the coroner and those who were present immediately after the two officers were shot. Suddenly, the defendant was intently listening to the observations of every witness. If he approved of the testimony or thought it favored him in any way, his face would alight with glee, but if he disapproved or the witness's statement was derogatory, he would sink in his chair, frowning.

As the defendant rose from the Defense table and headed to the witness stand, everyone in the audience keenly trained their attention to see what was going to happen.

Upon taking the stand and at the questioning of his attorney, J.D. Murphree, Anderson opened his testimony by saying that on the day of the killings of the two police officers, he had been in Brantley's pool hall shooting pool and that he had been drinking heavily. Later in the afternoon, he had gone to Hobbs's Soft Drink Stand, and when he came out, he was confronted by Patrolman Rittenberry, who, upon seeing Anderson, drew his revolver. "I asked him," testified Anderson, "'What do you want to kill me for?'"

Anderson went on to say that Rittenberry arrested him at that point. The witness continued, "Patrolman Purdy came up, and I gave him my knife and peacefully submitted to being arrested. But as we were walking across the street toward the police station, for no reason, Officer Rittenberry struck me in the ribs with his club and told me to take back what I had called him. Officer Purdy remonstrated him and told him to stop attacking me."

Murphree asked the defendant what he had called the officer. Anderson said he did not remember, and he said things were unclear to him at that point as he had been drinking beer and whiskey all day. "All I remember was being locked up at the station; I was freezing and asked for a fire to be lit."

Anderson continued, "I have always been friendly with the policemen in Shelbyville. Some time back, Officer Henry came to my livery and brought two beers he and I drank together."

He said, "When I was released from jail, I returned to my stables and found my horse had been bridled and attached to a buggy." (Here Anderson directly contradicted Searcy Rayburn's earlier testimony that Anderson had driven up in a buggy.)

Anderson continued, "I did not give any orders for this to be done. I then took the harness from the horse, unhitched it from the buggy, found a saddle and started to place it on the animal. Rayburn told me not to use that saddle, which would hurt the horse's back. I then went to Mullin's Stables next door to find a saddle. Before I got the saddle on the horse, my wife, knowing I intended to go to my father's house, came from our apartment upstairs and begged me not to leave. She was joined in her protest by Burris and Jones, who also advised me not to go. I intended to go to my father's home and left anyway."

J.D. Murphree asked, "Did you go to your father's house?"

Anderson replied, "No, I went to the house of Mrs. Eliza Baltimore, which is about a two-mile ride out the Wartrace dirt road. After staying with her for about a half to three-quarters of an hour, I left. I intended to proceed to my father's house but remembered that I had to be here in town the following day to answer the charges of being drunk, so I decided to return to Shelbyville. I intended to see Jim Hamilton. I wanted to talk to him about fixing it for me in court."

"As I rode into the outskirts of town, I came upon two men walking on the road in front of me. As I drew closer, I overheard the men talking and overheard one of them say, 'If they catch him, they'll mob him.' I was interested in what they were talking about, so I asked them to whom they were referring. 'Marion Anderson has shot two policemen in town and has run away,' was their reply. It was dark, and apparently, they did not recognize me and were unaware that it was me to whom they were referring. They went on to say that there were at least 50 men out looking for the killer, and if found, they would undoubtedly mob 'Anderson.'

"Rapidly turning my horse, I started to my father's house again. After riding a long distance, I realized that in the darkness, I had taken the wrong road and was not going toward my father's home. I found myself in the vicinity of (Walter) Hickerson's house. I stopped and knocked on the door. When he appeared, I told him I needed a place to stay and asked if I could sleep in his barn. He agreed. After stabling my horse, I told Mr. Hickerson what I had learned from the two men on the road into town and that I was now the subject of a search by a group of men looking to mob me."

"After spending the night in his corncrib, the following day I asked Hickerson if he would get me some cartridges because if there was a mob trying to kill me as the men had said, I was going to get a pistol from my brother as I did not have one myself."

Murphree asked, "How long did you stay at Mr. Hickerson's home?"

"I left that afternoon and went to my father's. I penned a letter from my father's house to Sheriff Williams telling him I would turn myself in as soon as the people quieted down," replied Anderson.

"And did you give yourself up?"

"On January 2nd, I sent for my attorney, Paul Myers, and at that time, I gave myself up voluntarily. I met Mr. Myers outside of town, and he took me to his house. While at Myers's home, Sheriff Rucker came up and arrested me. We requested that Squire Whitthorne be sent for instead of having me be bought into town. While waiting for the magistrate to come and arrange a preliminary hearing, Sheriff Williams arrived on the scene with a warrant for my arrest."

Attorney Murphree asked the defendant about his relationship with Searcy Rayburn, Anderson's cousin and an employee at the livery. Anderson stated that he had only employed the man and invited him to his home once for dinner. After that, Rayburn stayed because he was his cousin. Anderson stated that Rayburn helped in the livery, but most of his income was helping him sell wildcat whiskey. Anderson said he had found some of the whiskey in the gear room of the stables and that Rayburn had been selling the whiskey out of the lower part of that establishment.

In his final question to the defendant, Murphree asked, "Are you guilty of the murder of the policeman?"

In a loud declaration, Anderson stated, "I never killed nobody. I was at the house of Mrs. Baltimore at the time of the murder."

After questioning the defendant, Murphree sat down at the defense table and, cupping his hands around his mouth, said something to his co-counsel, Thomas Myers.

It was time for Attorney General Faulkner, the lead prosecutor, to cross-examine the defendant. He rose and approached Marion

Anderson. For the next several hours of cross-examination, Faulkner's questioning would be so sharp and to the point that it sometimes left the defendant rattled and uncomfortable.

Faulkner started his questioning by asking if it was true that Anderson had made no provisions for the safety and welfare of his wife and children or for carrying on the operations of his livery business before leaving for Coffee County. Anderson answered that he had left Searcy Rayburn in charge of the livery and his family. He added that he was sure both his family and the business were in capable hands.

"You must have had great confidence in Mr. Rayburn to bestow responsibility for your family and the operation of your business on him."

"Yes, I did."

"Mr. Anderson," continued Faulkner, "did you tell Mr. Rayburn you were leaving? Did you give him any instructions? Mr. Anderson, did you even tell your wife you were leaving? Did you say goodbye to Mrs. Anderson or your children?"

This question seemed to rock the defendant to his core.

Evasively, Anderson said, "I did not have to tell Rayburn anything; I knew I could trust that he would do a good job."

"Did you tell anyone goodbye?"

"I told Mrs. Baltimore I would not return for a while." Anderson's answer brought a resounding gasp from some and a laugh from others in the courtroom.

"Mr. Anderson, let me ask you. Did you check on your family and your business while you were in hiding?"

"I did keep informed of what was happening by talking to my attorney, Paul Myers, and my brother, with whom I was staying in the mountains."

"How did you make a living? What did you use for money between October when you left Shelbyville and January when you were arrested?"

This question rattled the defendant. With much trepidation, Anderson admitted, "I carried on my bootlegging business. I purchased the whiskey and then had Rayburn sell it out of the stable. I paid him some for selling the liquor and kept the rest."

Continuing his questioning, General Faulkner drilled the defendant, asking why it took two months to finally turn himself in to authorities. He also asked him about the statement he had made to his wife as he rode away from the livery on October 31st about "getting both of them"—about his relationship with Elizabeth Baltimore.

All the time that Marion Anderson had been on the stand, his wife Tennie, who had been sitting with him at the defense table, kept her eyes glued to his face; never once had she averted her eyes while he testified. Because of the configuration of the courtroom, this was the first time she had been able to watch his emotions and read his body language. It can only be assumed that she took a particular interest in his testimony as they pertained to his interactions with his mistress, Elizabeth Baltimore.

In the almost four and a half hours that the defendant was on the stand, he failed to make a confident witness in his own defense. It was apparent that Anderson had failed to convince the jury that he had been at the home of his lover at the time of the murders. Nor had he, as he had promised to do, shed a light on anyone else who was responsible for the events of Halloween night.

The prosecution refrained from asking the defendant any further questions, and he was excused from the witness stand.

The next witness for the defense was George Anderson (no relation to the defendant). This witness stated that on the night of the killing he had been deputized as a policeman. He said that since he did not own a weapon, he and another deputized man, Will Tindsley, were going to the houses of some friends in an attempt to borrow a gun. He went on to say that while out on the dirt road to Wartrace, he and Tindsley were talking about the murders when a horseman approached them from their rear. The man had overheard a part of their conversation and asked what was happening in the city. After they answered his question, the horseman swiftly turned his steed around and rode rapidly in the same direction from which he had just come.

Attorney Myers asked if the witness could describe the horse or rider who had approached them on that night of Halloween. He said he could not describe the horse's color or the rider because of the darkness at that hour.

"Would you be surprised to learn that the man mounted on the horse that night was the subject of your search, Marion Anderson?"

"If I had known that the man was Marion Anderson, I would have run," the witness responded.

George Anderson's testimony melted in cross-examination by T.N. Greer. Greer got the witness to admit that the moon was full and bright on the night of this encounter. He asked how it was that, as a policeman, he stood at most 15 feet from the man he was supposed to be searching for and did not recognize him. Because the lighting on the road that night was bright, how could he not even describe the horse's color as light yellow? He also pointed out that he had purchased whiskey from Marion Anderson several times. Again, he asked how it was that, from that distance, he did not recognize the man's voice.

The balance of the afternoon centered on a solid effort by the defense to break down the convincing testimony given by Searcy Rayburn for the State. Rayburn had formidable ties to the defendant, and it had been his damaging testimony that on the night the policemen were murdered, he witnessed Marion Anderson tie up his horse in front of the Stone and Hobbs Livery Stable and then disappear into the darkness. Rayburn heard four shots fired and, within a few minutes, saw Anderson run back to the livery, mount his waiting horse, and make his getaway.

Defense attorney Greer called to the stand W.H. Crowell (the public defender who had been the attorney for Neal, Greer, and Bomar in the murder of railroad detective Everson), E.H. Allen, and former Bedford County Sheriff W.G. Rucker, who had been members of the Coroner's jury in front of whom Rayburn had testified shortly after the murders. The defense tried to show that Rayburn had not presented the same testimony at the Coroner's inquiry that he later gave at the preliminary hearing and now in the trial at hand. When questioned, all three men said they could not remember the evidence or the circumstances presented well enough to say there had been a discrepancy in the testimonies.

Attorney Greer called Benton Anderson, the defendant's son, to the stand. The younger Anderson told the court that he had heard Rayburn threaten the police for spying on him at his work at the livery. He said Rayburn had even tried to borrow a pistol that he told him his father kept in a dresser drawer. Rayburn implied that he intended to use it against the officers.

The state's attorneys did not cross-examine Benton Anderson. Arthur Kizer, a boarder at the house of Mrs. Snoddy, who lived next door to the Stone and Hobbs Livery, was the next witness to be called to the stand for the defense. Attorney Myers, through this witness, wanted to establish a timeline in which the defendant could not have been the person who fatally wounded the two patrolmen.

On the stand, Kizer related that, watching from his bedroom window overlooking the stable, he saw a horseman ride up to the stables. When asked if he could tell who the man on the horse was, he said he identified the horseman as the defendant Marion Anderson, with whom he was quite familiar. He went on to say that as it was his bedtime, he turned and started toward his bed. He said he then heard four shots ring out. He dashed onto the roof of the house just outside his bedroom window. Kizer said, "At that time, I saw the horseman sitting below me and in front of the stable. As soon as I climbed out my window and onto the roof, the horseman turned his horse and rode away."

During cross-examination, prosecuting attorney Greer sharply attacked the witness about his statement. "Mr. Kizer, you said that you quickly ran back to your window and out onto the roof of Mrs. Snoddy's home. You said it was only a matter of seconds for you to accomplish that feat. Is that correct?"

"Yes, that is correct."

"But isn't it true that you did not immediately return to the window? Isn't it true that you had dozed off to sleep only to be awakened by the shots, and it was only after you roused from your slumber that you went to the roof to ascertain what had happened?"

"Yes, I guess you are right," admitted Kizer.

"So, Mr. Kizer, can you tell the court exactly how much time had elapsed from when you first saw the man on horseback and when you saw him ride away? It could have been a matter of one, two, or even several minutes. Isn't that right?"

"Yes, sir, it could have been."

After Arthur Kizer was excused from the witness stand, Judge Richardson adjourned the trial for the day. It would resume at 8:00 a.m. the following day.

With the conclusion of testimony on Tuesday the 16th, Thomas Myers approached Judge Richardson with a special request. He asked if he might take the defendant to his office and plan a strategy for defending him the following day.

Judge Richardson immediately dismissed any notion from Myers that he could get the defendant to a private office. Richardson told him that such a request would not fall under his jurisdiction. Instead, his request would fall under the purview of Sheriff Williams. When the attorney approached the sheriff to ask if he might bring the defendant to his office, he was quickly denied his request. The sheriff told Myers he would make accommodations for him to meet his client in the jail, but under no circumstances would the sheriff expend the manpower to provide for a meeting outside the confines of the jail.

As newspapers in Nashville and Chattanooga went to print on the morning of the 17th of April, the consensus in their reports was that General Faulkner and his associates for the prosecution had won the battle over the opposing team of J.D. Murphree and the father-son team of Thomas and Paul Myers. But newspapers did not hand down verdicts. It would be up to the jury to determine which of the sides had been more convincing.

Wednesday, April 17, 1912, Day Three of the Trial

Security had been tight on the morning of the 15th, It was even more so on the second and third days of the trial. The sheriff's office was receiving threats against the defendant, and the deputies were making sure that there would not be a repeat of the incident that occurred in the courthouse when in January, three Negro prisoners were attacked, and two of them had been killed. There was no doubt there were many in Bedford County who would lynch Marion Anderson if given the opportunity.

The entire week of April 15th was stormy. The fields in the county were saturated with rain, and the local farmers were unable to work their farms. However, the wet conditions allowed many of them to forego farm work and come into town to observe the trial … and many did.

As Judge Richardson gaveled the proceedings into session, the courtroom was filled to capacity, and approximately 200 want-to-be spectators lined the stairs and hallway of the courthouse.

Before the morning's opening arguments and before the jurors were brought into the courtroom, defense counsel approached the judge to enter a complaint. Attorney Murphree brought to Judge Richardson an accusation that one of the defense's primary witnesses had been tampered with. He said that representatives of a Shelbyville corporation had offered the witness money to withhold evidence that would acquit their client.

When asked how this information had come to Mr. Murphree's attention, it was revealed that the accusation of tampering had come through the defendant's wife, Tennie.

This may have been a ploy by the defense team because they could introduce this evidence by saying it was through Mrs. Anderson, knowing that the prosecution could not force her to the stand to testify against her husband.

Judge Richardson took the complaint under advisement but dismissed it for lack of evidence.

On this, the third day of the trial, the prosecution continued presenting their argument; attempting to strengthen their case, the State called five more witnesses. The first to be called was Mrs. H.C. Ryall. Mrs. Ryall lived just 40 feet from the stables where Anderson was the proprietor. She was called to relate what she had heard and seen on the night of the murders.

Taking the witness stand, she recalled that on that Halloween night in 1911, she was carrying some flowers to her front door when she heard the report of four gunshots coming from the vicinity of the courthouse square. Thinking it was a fire alarm, she said she waited for the fire whistle to sound, but it did not. She went on to say that while still standing in her front yard, she heard the sound of hoofbeats on the pavement departing from the area of the stables and then saw a horse and rider gallop quickly past her house. She said they were headed north toward Wartrace.

The defense asked this witness a couple of questions, and then she was dismissed from the witness stand.

Recalled then to the stand was J.E. Burris, who had testified on the first day of the trial. Burris was recalled so that he could relate, one more time, that he had heard Anderson say that the police had mistreated him and he was, "going to kill some of the people who arrested him."

Next to be called to the witness stand was Mrs. George W. Snoddy, who lived across the street from the livery. She said she saw a woman come down from the upstairs apartment above the stables before the shots were fired and then heard a woman scream: "O, Daddy! O, Daddy!"

Defense attorney Thomas Myers, on cross-examination, tried to get Mrs. Snoddy to say that the scream had come from farther up the street near the butcher shop in front of which the shootings had occurred. Still, Mrs. Snoddy was adamant that the cry had come from in front of the stables.

Mrs. Snoddy was followed to the stand by Mrs. E.C. Halmantaler, the wife of the butcher in front of whose shop the ambush had taken place. Mrs. Halmantaler stated that she heard the approaching footsteps of the two police officers, four shots, and then the sound of someone running away toward the Stone and Hobbs Livery.

Following Mrs. Halmantaler was H.M. McAdams, a carpenter, who was working in Haggard's Barber Shop that night. He said that he, too, overheard the defendant threaten the police because they had run a woman with whom he was intimate out of town.

A late addition to the list of those to testify was H.C. Ryall, whose wife had testified earlier. Judge Richardson had allowed the defense to call the witness late in the trial because Ryall had just arrived back in Shelbyville the night before after being absent for over a month. Attorney Myers called the witness to discredit the testimony of S.M. Rayburn, the prosecution's chief witness. Myers was disappointed that the witness's testimony echoed almost verbatim what his wife had said when she was on the stand. Ryall said he heard the horse's hoofbeats striking the pavement as it left the front of the stables next door on the night of the murders. He stated he also heard the screams of a woman but could not distinguish what the woman had said.

With the completion of this testimony, the court adjourned its morning session. The judge called for the trial to reconvene after a lunch break.

When the afternoon session was gaveled into order, Sheriff Williams took the stand and stated that as soon as he learned of the murders, he had deputized every Bedford County citizen willing to take up arms and give chase to the defendant. He added that he had printed circulars publicizing the $1,000 bounty offered for Anderson's apprehension and conviction. "I never gave up until the defendant was captured on January 2nd," testified Sheriff Williams.

The last two witnesses to testify in the trial were John Powell, a former deputy sheriff from Coffee County, and H.R. Summers, a retired sheriff from Coffee County. Throughout the trial, the defense attorneys had attempted to impugn the character of S.M. Rayburn, the prosecution's star witness. The state's attorney introduced these two as character witnesses. Both men testified that they had known Rayburn for several years and had known him to have a good reputation.

This concluded the testimony of the witnesses. It was time for closing arguments.

Judge Richardson admonished both sides that their closings would be limited to three hours each. He also gave the attorneys a synopsis of the deliberation instructions he would present to the jury when he charged them. In this way, the attorneys could comment on the jury instructions in their closing arguments.

Closing arguments for the defense were presented by lead attorney Thomas Myers.

In his closing statement, Myers began, "The seriousness of this case presents to the mind the feebleness and frailties of human nature." Regarding the murder, he said it was utterly impossible to explain, except there were one of two theories: "The man must have been either a lunatic or a straightforward, cool-headed murderer."

He thanked the people of Bedford County for their attention during the trial and for being content to leave the case in the hands of the law, a clear nod of the head to these people that they had not dragged his client from the control of the sheriff and lynched him from one of the lampposts of Shelbyville.

In an attempt to shift the focus of the murder from his client, Marion Anderson, Myers went on to speak to the fact that the body of the slain policemen was found only a few feet from the door of Mr. Halmantaler's shop. If the jury were going to convict Mr. Anderson on circumstantial evidence, why could those same circumstances not point just as easily to Mr. Halmantaler? Myers alluded to Daniel Webster's famous oratory of the 1830s when acting as a prosecuting attorney against the accused murder of a Captain White in Salem, Massachusetts. In his closing argument, Webster cited "Murder Will Out" (from an 1830 ruling by the Massachusetts Supreme Court in the trial of Joseph Knapp and George Crowninshield for the murder of Captain Joseph White) and convinced the jury that the man on trial had motive and opportunity and was in the proximity of the victim at the time of the murder. Myers's supposition was that anyone other than the defendant, Anderson, could have perpetrated the murder.

Paul Myers approached the jury box. Steely-eyed in his approach, Myers pleaded ardently for the life of his client. With eloquence, the attorney tried to make plain to the jurors the plausibility of the story that had been presented to them by the defense. He said, "Mr. Anderson was not even in Shelbyville at the time of this terrible incident. My client did not commit this murder."

His comment then turned to the defendant's cousin, S.M. Rayburn.

"Regarding the prosecution's star witness, gentlemen, S.M. Rayburn is a liar and has perjured himself." Myers clarified that he did not respect or believe in anything Rayburn had stated in court. He then listed points from Rayburn's testimony that the attorney said were inconsistent with what he said he had been given during the Coroner's inquest.

He ended by advising the jury about a conviction that the Tennessee Supreme Court had reversed on account of circumstantial evidence. In closing, he said, "The fate of the defendant is now in your hands, and we must have a fair and impartial trial, for that is what our religion, the word of Christ, teaches us, as well as our English law. As you love your God, put away all sentiments, close your eyes, and be influenced by the blind goddess, Lady Justice. By all means, gentlemen of the jury, do not hang a man on evidence of a perjurer."

When Myers closed his statement, co-defense Attorney Murphree rose to address the jury. Murphree, in his summation, pointed out that the defendant was an alcoholic but not a killer, and in fact, he pointed out that the defendant was a friend to both Officer Henry and Officer Purdy. His primary defense was that at the time of the murder, his client was not even in the city of Shelbyville. He reminded the jury that his client had ridden out of town heading for his father's farm, stopping at Mrs. Baltimore's home on the city's outskirts. He pointed out that at the time of the shots being fired, he was several miles away. As far as Anderson staying hidden from authorities and not turning himself—well, that was because Marion Anderson feared for his life.

Using his last opportunity to address the jury and in an attempt to cast a modicum of doubt that his client was the guilty party, Attorney Murphree said, "Gentlemen of the jury, I can assure you that Marion Anderson did not commit this murder for he is too brave—he would fight a regiment—but it was some person who had slipped from behind and done this dastardly deed."

And with that, the defense rested its case.

In a criminal trial, the prosecution always has the burden of proof. This is why the prosecution speaks last in closing arguments.

General Faulkner rose from the table and walked toward the jury box containing the 12 Bedford County farmers. Unbuttoning his suit coat jacket, he began his statement.

The defendant's entire family watched Faulkner's every move and hung on every word. Anderson's sister sat at the bar just to the left and behind where the defendant sat. To his right sat his brother, and beside him at the defense table, looking pale and haggard, sat his wife Tennie. Anderson sat through the appeal to the jury, his eyes never leaving the face of the attorney general throughout the entire one-and-a-half hour closing arguments.

In a staccato cadence, Faulkner enunciated the following: "Gentlemen, Shelbyville Police Officer R.G. Purdy is dead, and the defendant in this case, Marion Anderson, is guilty of murdering him." He wanted to drive forcefully into the minds of each of the jurors the fact that the defendant and only this defendant was guilty of taking the life of one of the city's finest.

General Faulkner reminded the jury of the essential steps that had brought everyone in the courtroom to this place. Then, point by point, he began to expose the flaws in the story Anderson had presented in his defense.

As the attorney moved forward to deliver his closing remarks, a somber silence fell upon those in the courtroom, particularly when General Faulkner began talking about Elizabeth Baltimore, the woman with whom the defendant was supposedly intimate.

Rain from the heavy storm that had been inundating Shelbyville for the last three days noisily beat against the courtroom windows. Claps of thunder and a deluge of water pelting the windows made it hard to hear what was being said. Raising his voice to overcome the noise of the storm, Faulkner continued, "Gentlemen of the jury, my learned opponent would have you think that the defendant was miles away from the city when this officer was killed. He would have you believe that Marion Anderson was making a social visit to a woman the defendant himself admits to being his long-time mistress. The State has proven to you through the testimony of several witnesses that the defendant had just departed Stone and Hobbs Livery only minutes before the shots were heard, and this same defendant ran back to the livery, mounted a horse, and rode away into the darkness just moments after the shots rang out. Please recall the testimony of Mrs. H.C. Ryall and Mrs. George Snoddy, who both said the defendant, Marion Anderson, rode away from the livery at a galloping pace after the shots were fired. I want you to recall the testimony of Mr. J.E. Burris and Mr. H.M. McAdams, who told you that they heard the defendant threaten the lives of the policemen who had arrested him earlier on the day of the murder."

"Let me remind you that not only has Marion Anderson broken the laws of man and God by perpetrating this murder, breaking the sixth commandment, but here also sits the defendant admitting his relations with a woman, not his wife, and in doing so, has broken the seventh commandment as well.

"Gentlemen, I come before you with a man as guilty a criminal as has ever stood before 12 good men and true, and as your representative, I ask you boldly to bring in a verdict of murder in the first degree."

Judge Richardson gaveled the trial closed. As the hour was growing late and wanting to give the jury a fresh start on which to deliberate, he closed the proceedings for the day and set the trial to resume at 8:30 a.m. the following morning.

After receiving instructions from Judge Richardson, jury deliberations began at 11:00 a.m. on Friday. Most of those who had been following the trial expected a swift verdict. The jury was expected to deliberate for only a few minutes, probably an hour at maximum. When they had not returned in two hours, the crowd became restless. After three hours had passed and the jury had not finished deliberations, rumors of a hung jury and a mistrial began to be murmured throughout the crowd.

Seven hours later, at 6:00 p.m., they had not reached a verdict. The jury foreman sent word to the judge, telling him that, in his opinion, they would not be able to reach a verdict even if they were to remain sequestered into the evening. He reported to Judge Richardson that it had been a very long day and requested permission to adjourn and go to their homes for the evening.

The judge agreed to the request, telling them that deliberations could restart the following morning.

The court convened at 8:30 a.m. on Saturday. At 11:15 a.m., the jury passed a note stating that they had reached a decision in the case.

All parties in the case were summoned, and the jury was brought into the courtroom. The foreperson rose and faced the judge. Judge Richardson queried, "Have you reached a verdict in this case?"

"We have, your honor. In the case of the State of Tennessee against Marion E. Anderson on the charge of the murder of Police Officer R.G. Purdy, we find the defendant guilty in the second degree."

With the declaration from the jury foreman, a collective gasp echoed through the courtroom both from the friends of the defendant, who were sure that the jury would never vote to convict Anderson, and from those who were sure the jury would convict on the original charge of first-degree murder.

Upon hearing the verdict, Paul Myers asked for the jury to be polled. Each member of the jury answered that their verdict was to find the defendant guilty of the charge of second-degree murder.

Upon hearing that he was facing a lengthy prison term, Marion Anderson, who had been upbeat entering the proceeding that morning, suddenly looked haggard and defeated.

It was later discovered that before the jury came to a unanimous vote of second-degree murder, they had initially split, with seven men voting for first-degree murder, three for second-degree murder, and two men voting for acquittal. The second-degree conclusion was a compromise to come to a verdict.

Immediately after the jury's verdict was delivered, Judge Richardson turned to the trial's sentencing phase. A first-degree conviction for the murder of a policeman would have carried a mandatory death penalty; the second-degree conviction carried a lesser sentence of 20 years in the Tennessee penitentiary, with the possibility of parole.

The judge thanked the jurors for their service and told the defendant and his attorney to stand. "Sir, you have been convicted by a jury of your peers with one count of second-degree murder. Under the guidelines set forth by the criminal code for the State of Tennessee, I, therefore, sentence you to a term of 20 years in the Tennessee State Penitentiary."

Anderson showed little emotion as he listened to the judge's decree.

He looked over at his wife sitting beside him at the defendant's table. Tennie began to weep silently as she heard the judge's words.

Tennie, who had been cast aside for another woman, had sat bravely supporting her husband. Unflinchingly, she had endured the pain of listening to the details of his infidelity and the double life he had inflicted on her, and yet her devotion never wavered.

Tennie's resolve to support her man had so disarmed her husband that he broke down at the end of the trial and admitted that he had wronged her. He asked her forgiveness and declared he would do everything he could to support his wife and children during his imprisonment.

After finishing his pronouncement, Judge Richardson asked the defendant if he wished to make a statement. "Yes, Your Honor," said Anderson. He rose from his chair and addressed everyone in the room. "I am not guilty of this hideous crime for which I have wrongly been found guilty. I was not in the city when the murders occurred."

When first brought to justice, Anderson had maintained that he had enemies who had killed the officers and had set him up to take the fall. Still, by the time he was brought to trial, he had changed his story to say that he could not have been the culprit because, at the time of the shootings, he was in the arms of his paramour. He never mentioned the supposed enemies again.

Chapter Seven

The Second Trial of Marion Anderson

Monday, July 1, 1912, Shelbyville, Tennessee

Marion Anderson, already convicted and sentenced to 20 years in the state penitentiary for the murder of Officer Redin G. Purdy, was now about to stand trial again for the murder of Officer Charles Henry.

Initially, a trial date in the matter of the murder of Officer Henry had been agreed upon by defense attorney Thomas Myers and the prosecuting attorneys for May 27th. But after the end of the first trial and before the start of the second, the Myers legal team resigned as Anderson's attorneys. A new law office headed by Nashville attorney H.C. Shimer assumed the role of his defending attorneys. By the time Shimer and his associate attorneys got up to speed, it became apparent the trial date of May 27th would result in extreme hardship for the new attorneys, who would not have had time to mount a proper defense. Shimer petitioned Judge Richardson to obtain a continuance in late May, just days before the trial was to have commenced. After consulting with the prosecuting attorney, the judge consented to the request. A new trial date of July 1st was assigned.

Before the first trial, Captain D.A. Curtis, clerk of the jury commission, had prepared a list of 650 potential jury members for Judge Richardson. Given the notoriety raised by the first trial, the second trial's jury pool would have to be much more extensive to find impartial jurors. The sensitivity of the first trial left few citizens of the county without at least a rudimentary familiarity with what had happened the night of October 31st, and most of those persons had formed an opinion on the guilt or innocence of the defendant. This familiarity turned out to be an almost impossible hurdle to overcome. The vetting of the hundreds of potential veniremen started at 9:00 a.m. on the first morning of the second trial.

Since his conviction for the murder of Officer Purdy, Anderson had been taken back to Nashville and housed for safekeeping in the Davidson County Jail. The night before the second trial began, Sheriff Williams and two of his deputies were dispatched to bring the prisoner back to Shelbyville. Upon leaving Nashville, Anderson had little to say other than that he was confident that this second trial would result in a favorable outcome for himself.

As before, security for the trial was of the utmost importance. Sheriff's deputies were stationed throughout the courthouse, and everyone had to undergo an extensive search before entering.

This second trial would bring no less excitement, no less curiosity, and no abatement of the indignation felt by the citizens of Shelbyville concerning the murder of two of their policemen, a crime considered by most Bedford County citizens to be one of the most horrid ever perpetrated in the city. Realizing the temperament of the community, and because of the lynching in this same courthouse, just five months before, of murder suspects Dave Neal and Wat Greer, and the attempted lynching of David Bomar, Judge Richardson had ordered the defendant returned to the security and sequestration of the county jail in Nashville. Indeed, no one in Shelbyville, especially Sheriff Williams, wanted a repeat of the events of February 19th. Therefore, since the first trial, Anderson had been returned to Davidson County for safekeeping.

At 8:35 a.m., Anderson entered the courtroom on the second floor of the Bedford County Courthouse. Taking his place at the defense table, he did not seem quite as assured or cocky as he had been on the first day of the Purdy trial. Anderson was suffering from a lack of sleep. He had not been returned from Nashville to the Bedford County jail until after 11:00 p.m. on Sunday and had not gotten settled enough to sleep until the wee hours of the morning.

Voir dire (jury selection) began at 9:00 a.m. At 11:45 a.m., Judge Richardson recessed jury selection for a lunch break. When the court reconvened at 1:00 p.m., the attorneys announced a significant development in the case. During the break, Attorney General Walter Faulkner and Attorney Shimer had conferenced, and the district attorney had offered Anderson a plea agreement. Rather than have the state try the defendant for a second time, General Faulkner offered to allow Anderson to plead to the offense of the second-degree murder of Officer Henry in exchange for a 20-year sentence. This sentence would run consecutively to the punishment given to him for the murder of Officer Purdy. The DA seemed to think that 40 years for a defendant in his 30s was a life sentence and would satisfy those who wanted a severe punishment for the defendant.

During jury deliberation at his first trial, Marion Anderson had narrowly escaped the death penalty. This fact was not lost on the defendant and his attorneys, and if anything, instead of subsiding, the ill feelings against him by the citizens of Bedford County had intensified since then. Attorney Shimer monitored the community's sentiments between the trials, and signs of hostilities had risen considerably. Afraid he might get a jury that would vote for the death penalty, Shimer did not want to have to go through the second trial and have the jury send his client to the gallows.

Anderson, at first, was adamant that he did not want to accept the plea deal. Always cocky and self-assured that he would be found innocent of the charges, he refused the offer. The attorney assured him that he could be out of prison in fifteen years under the current sentencing guidelines if he accepted the plea. More importantly, at least for the time being, Shimer reminded his client that, with hostility mounting among the citizens of the county, there was a good chance someone in Shelbyville might well attempt to shoot him if he stayed in Bedford County for a trial.

Armed with this information and with Anderson understanding that if convicted, he was facing death by hanging,[6] Shimer was able to convince his client to accept the offer.

When the plea agreement was read, the courtroom was packed with spectators. A significant murmur was heard throughout the room when those in attendance realized that the proceedings were ending and that there would not be a trial.

Sheriff Williams was notified that the defendant had chosen not to go to trial and that he needed to summon an automobile to dispatch the prisoner immediately back to Nashville. Anderson kissed his wife goodbye, and he was gone from her within minutes. About 40 deputies immediately sealed the doors to the courtroom and lined the hallway leading to the waiting car.

Marion Anderson was out of the city and well on his way to Nashville before those sequestered in the courtroom were allowed to leave.

Under normal circumstances, the prisoner would have been taken back to the Davidson County Jail. Instead, after a long-distance call to Nashville, it was decided that Anderson would be taken directly to the penitentiary for processing. The three-and-a-half hour drive from Shelbyville made their arrival at the state pen too late for the inmate to be processed into the system. Anderson was placed in a holding cell, and the following morning, he was processed as inmate #6521 and put in the White men's wing of the prison.

---

[6] In 1912, the means of lethal execution in Tennessee was hanging. The Tennessee legislature would not introduce the electric chair as the manner of execution until September 1913, and its first use would not be until 1916.

As a follow-up to the story of the Shelbyville trial, there was an article in the *Lawrence Democrat* (Lawrenceburg, Tennessee) dated July 17th. The article reported that Anderson has acclimated to his new prisoner role after almost three weeks of incarceration. He was keeping to himself and had requested the warden that he be assigned to a job in the facility that paid the most for his labor. Anderson, who, before committing the murders, had almost abandoned his wife for a mistress, had decided to do everything within his power to support his wife and children now that he was separated from them.

Chapter Eight

Aftermath

Charles Wat Greer was killed by the lynch mob on February 20, 1912, as he and his two co-defendants in the murder of railroad detective Everson were exiting the courtroom of the Bedford County Courtroom.

Wat Greer is buried in an unknown location in Bedford County.

Dave Neal was shot during the lynching of his half-brother, Wat Greer. Dave's luck would finally run out on March 11, 1912, when he died from the gunshot wound he incurred three weeks before on the day of the lynching.

The man who had over the years been shot four times, two of which had been shots to his head, and who had sustained several lesser wounds in the foot and hand resulting from all the fights and stints he had been involved in, did not survive the last assault.

An article in the *Chattanooga Daily Times* stated that the wounds Neal sustained on February 19th had been fatal. Neal, who was once quoted as saying, "There is not a God-damned White man that can kill me," had died at the hands of a lynch mob consisting of White men.

Dave Neal is buried in an unknown grave in Bedford County.

Charles Dane Bomar not only survived the attack perpetrated on him and his two co-defendants, but he went on to live a long and productive life. Though initially charged in connection with the murder of Detective Everson, prosecutors determined his role in the proceedings aboard the train had not been as central in the detective's fate as that of Neal and Greer. After the attempt on his life by the lynch mob, all charges were dismissed in August of 1912. With the death of his co-defendants, there was no one left to try for the murder of Detective Everson.

A short time after his release by the sheriff's department, Bomar moved away from the county. Dane Bomar's time with the NC&St.L Ry. was over. It would have been impossible for him to continue his employment with the railroad, working side-by-side with men who might continue to hold a grudge. His near-death experience with a lynch mob certainly indicated that it would be prudent to get as far away from Bedford County as possible. At the time, Bomar had family and friends in Cincinnati, Ohio. He moved to that city and worked several jobs as a laborer for the next few years. On June 5, 1917, 27-year-old Dane Bomar and a friend walked into a military recruitment office in Cincinnati and signed enlistment papers that would induct Bomar as a soldier in the U.S. Army. He would serve during World War I, assigned to the Services of Supply section of the American Expeditionary Forces, like most Black men who went to war. This section was comprised of stevedore, labor, and engineering service battalions and companies. The primary function of these units was to support and provide materials to other companies along the front.

After completing his military service, Bomar returned to Chattanooga and embarked on a lengthy career with the Southern Railway. He was an active Sunday school teacher and deacon at his local church. He passed away in October 1969 at the age of 81.

Marion Anderson was not, as he predicted, able to convince a jury of his innocence during his trial for the murder of Shelby Police Officer Purdy, and he was sentenced to the Tennessee State Penitentiary for a term of 20 years. For the murder of the second policeman, Officer Henry, Anderson pleaded guilty to a charge of second-degree murder and received another 20-year sentence. The two sentences were to run consecutively, meaning he would not be released from custody until 1952 without time off for good behavior.

The convicted Anderson entered the prison gates on July 1, 1912.

The penitentiary ledger summarized the inmate's attributes quite concisely. Marion Anderson was a 33-year-old White male, 5'8" tall, and 153 pounds. He had blue eyes, black hair, and several scars on his face and forehead. His station of life was married. His trade (occupation) was listed as none, his education was limited, and he professed no religion.

Marion Anderson did not serve the 40 years for which he was convicted. He was released from the Tennessee State Penitentiary the first week of December 1926 after serving 14 years of that 40-year sentence. In November 1921, Tennessee Governor Albert H. Roberts commuted the first of his two sentences to time served and then pardoned him on the second conviction for the murder of Officer Henry.

Anderson lived to the age of 74, dying in 1953. He is buried in Manchester, Tennessee.

Sheriff James Henry "Big Jim" Williams served the citizens of Bedford County as sheriff from 1910 to 1912 and was re-elected for a second term from 1914 to 1918.

Jim always told friends he was a farmer first and a sheriff second. After his second term, he bought a larger farm in Linden, Alabama, and farmed it until his death in 1932 at the age of 68.

The Death of Harvey Spears In a sad footnote to the manhunt for Marion Anderson, on November 15, 1911, 13-year-old Harvey Spears, a resident of Manchester, Tennessee, was playing in the backyard of the family farm with his two younger brothers. Shouting out to them, Harvey said he wanted to demonstrate what would happen to Anderson after he was captured. The boy threw one end of a bridle reins over the limb of a tree and then tied the other end around his neck. The boy ran around in circles under the tree when he stumbled and fell. The two brothers ran to Harvey and attempted to lift their older sibling, but to no avail. One of the boys grabbed a chair and tried to dislodge the straps from the limb. This effort also failed. Noticing Harvey's deadly pallor, with alarm, the boys called to their mother to come from the house. Mrs. Spears found the lifeless boy still entangled in the restraints; the fall had broken his neck. A doctor was summoned, and upon his arrival, young Harvey was pronounced dead.

The Bedford County Courthouse Unfortunately, the lynching of Wat Greer and Dave Neal in 1912 would not be the last tragedy involving the courthouse. In December 1934, the courthouse built in 1873 was burned to the ground when an angry mob descended on the structure. The mob was set on the destruction of the courthouse when it was learned that E.K. Harris, a 22-year-old Black man who had been on trial for the sexual assault of a 14-year-old White girl, had been clandestinely removed from the building and taken away from Shelbyville for his safety.

Three attempts to invade the courthouse and carry off Harris were thwarted by a group of five hundred guardsmen on hand to protect the defendant. On the last assault, gasoline was poured around the foundation of the building, and within the hour, the building was no more. Before the incident was concluded, there were four dead and several others wounded at the hands of the guardsmen.

The current Bedford County Courthouse (of Classical Revival design) was constructed in 1935.

Chapter Nine

A History of Lynching in America

lynch | lin(t)SH | verb [with object] 1 (of a mob) kill (someone), especially by hanging, for an alleged offense with or without a legal trial.

—*New Oxford American Dictionary*

The term "Lynch mob" originated in America during the American Revolution when a Virginia justice of the peace named Charles Lynch, a Patriot, ordered extralegal punishment for Loyalists.

Lynching in Colonial America

The practice of hanging and lynching has been deeply ingrained in the history of America since the first colonists arrived on this continent. The first recorded instance of hanging as punishment for a crime occurred in 1630, when John Billington, one of the original Pilgrims who arrived on the Mayflower ten years before, was charged with the murder of another settler, John Newcomen. An angry mob of pilgrims captured Billington and hanged him without a formal trial.

Two years later, in 1632, America recorded the hanging of Jane Champion, a woman. Champion was brought to the Virginia colony around 1620 as part of a group of potential wives for wealthy landowners looking for a mate. She married Percival Champion, but in 1630, she had an affair with another colonist, Willi Gallopin. As a result of the affair, Jane became pregnant. She and Willi concealed the pregnancy and then murdered the child. The concealment of an unplanned pregnancy was an abominable sin under Puritan standards; the discovery of the murder brought a verdict of death for both parties.

In Nathaniel Hawthorne's *The Scarlet Letter,* the fictitious Hester Prynne is forced to wear a scarlet "A" for her indiscretions. Champion's punishment was much more severe: she was hanged. Gallopin somehow escaped execution.

The practice of lynching has often been associated with the lack of an efficient system of law enforcement on the American frontier. As a result, people were forced to take the law into their own hands. This self-reliance can partially explain why lynching and mob violence expanded in early America, but it is not the only factor. Two additional things to consider are the introduction of slavery, which brings a racial element, and the general spirit of anti-authoritarianism. Many early immigrants to America sought to escape religious persecution or oppressive government rule. For instance, Scottish and Irish settlers who came to America had experienced decades of infighting and persecution at the hands of the English. The same determination to fight against oppression and authoritarianism in their home countries continued after they arrived in America. This rebellion against authoritarian rule would give rise to the American colonists throwing off the mantle of British rule in the 1770s, splitting the country into two factions, North and South, during the War Between the States, and thousands of protests against local and state and national governments up to this day.

In the colonies, religion heavily influenced the concept of justice. The early settlers often viewed crimes as sins. From a religious perspective, offenders were seen as not only breaking the law but also violating God's commandments, which could bring punishment to the entire community. Punishing sinners was believed to restore divine order within the individual and the community. The drive to purify the community of sin became especially strong in the 1640s. It continued through the 1690s, a period marked by a significant increase in the hanging of women due to the onset of the witchcraft trials.

On a broader front, the relationship between the colonies and Britain's Crown became increasingly strained after the Mother Country enforced repressive acts such as the Tea Act (1773), the Quartering Act (1765), and the Townshend Acts (1767). Resistance to these Acts grew into mob action and was a driving force of colonial opposition.

Leading up to the American Revolution, tax collectors, customs officials, and merchants loyal to the Crown were targeted by mobs. These Tories were often whipped, pelted with rocks and eggs, and tarred and feathered. The mobs also destroyed the property of those not supporting the revolutionary cause, such as during the Boston Tea Party. Stores were ransacked and burned, printing presses destroyed, and shipments disrupted.

In 1775, Patrick Henry delivered his powerful "Give Me Liberty or Give Me Death" speech before the Virginia Assembly. This speech sparked outrage among those who had long distrusted totalitarianism. It led to a call to arms and set the stage for the American Revolution. The same men who had revolted against Britain's oppressive Tea, Quartering, and Townsend Acts, were the same men who raised the cry for freedom after Henry's speech. With sentiments against the Crown reaching a fever pitch, it was easy to understand how such a call to arms was quickly taken up.

During the post-Revolution period, White men were commonly hanged for war-related crimes such as spying, espionage, treason, or desertion. On the other hand, Black slaves were often hanged at the discretion of their owners, primarily for reasons officially labeled as revolt, although it could have been for any cause. Additionally, White individuals who showed sympathy towards slaves were also frequently hanged.

With no formal criminal justice system in place in the last quarter of the 18th century, vigilantism expanded exponentially. Citizens from communities banded together to become the "law" as they saw it.

Slave Codes

The ownership of human chattel began in America in the mid-1600s. The first English colony in the western hemisphere to establish slave codes was Barbados in 1661, marking the start of the legal codification of slavery. Because British common law did not recognize slavery as a legal institution, slave owners created their own set of rules governing the ownership of their slaves and their actions.

The code described Black people as heathenish, brutish, and uncertain—a dangerous kind of people. Most slave codes concerned the rights and duties of free people regarding enslaved individuals. Slave codes left a great deal unsaid, with much of the actual practice of slavery being a matter of tradition rather than formal law.

The Barbados slave code supposedly aimed to protect enslaved people from harsh treatment, but it provided minimal protection. The codes required owners to supply a few trivial provisions but not even the fundamental human rights as set out under common law. The code did, however, fix the institution of slavery as lifelong and inheritable, meaning that any child born to a slave woman was considered at birth to be a slave as well. They also protected masters from violence perpetrated against them by their slaves and outlined rules governing the handling of runaways. In North Carolina, the 1709 slave code went so far as to spell out who could and could not purchase an enslaved person.

> [N]o individuals, such as Negroes, mulattos, Indians, Jews, Moors, Muslims, or other non-Christians, will be allowed to purchase Christian servants. If any person from the groups mentioned above purchases a Christian white servant, that servant will automatically become free.

These draconian codes dictated a much harsher punishment for Black offenders than would have been inflicted on any White person charged with the same crime. Corporal punishment for Blacks could be harsh and included whipping, branding, castration, nose splitting, and the amputation of body parts.

The 1712 South Carolina slave code established the hierarchy of the state's racial groups. "Negroes and other enslaved people brought unto the people of this Province for that purpose are of barbarous, wild, savage natures, and as such renders them wholly unqualified to be governed by the laws, customs, and practices of this Province." When the British colonies of South Carolina, Georgia, and Virginia wanted to create laws governing their property, they used the Barbados codes as a model.

Immigrants often entered indentured servitude contracts of their own free will, as opposed to enslaved people who did not. Over one-half of all European immigrants to the American colonies between the 1630s and the American Revolution came under indentures.

The first arrival of African slaves in the 13 colonies can be traced back to 1619, when a passing slave ship en route to sugar plantations in the Caribbean landed in Virginia. Locals desperately needed laborers to work large plantations, so they purchased several Africans."

By 1790, the number of enslaved people in America was approaching three-quarters of a million persons. Countless numbers of those had successfully escaped bondage in the slave states and had made their way into states and territories where slavery had been abolished. To that point, no laws governed the mandatory return of property (slaves) to their owners. This lack of formal law brought the rise of slave patrols whose mission was to capture and return the runaways. Many of those who participated in the patrols were the same persons who would have been members of vigilante mobs in the past.

Due to concerns about growing slave populations and the risk of foreign invasion, Southerners established and later expanded slave patrols. South Carolina formed the first slave patrol in 1704 to capture runaways and address threats from Native Americans and the Spanish. These patrols, organized by the community, were later associated with mob violence and hunts for African Americans. These slave patrols were not unusual in colonial societies, as professional police departments were not established. Therefore, law enforcement was considered the responsibility of the entire community. The return of runaway slaves from the jurisdiction to which they had escaped soon became a legal and logistical nightmare. As late as the end of the 18th century, no existing laws governed the return of runaway property.

In stepped the Federal government.

In 1793, the U.S. House of Representatives enacted the Fugitive Slave Act, which affected the Constitution's Fugitive Slave Clause (1789).

The Fugitive Slave Clause is Article IV, Section 2, Clause 3 of the U.S. Constitution. It read:

> No Person held to Service or Labour in one State, under the Laws thereof, escaping into another, shall, in consequence of any Law or Regulation therein, be discharged from such Service or Labour, but shall be delivered up on Claim of the Party to whom such Service or Labour may be due.

The Fugitive Slave Clause guaranteed a slaveholder's right to recover an escaped enslaved person. It sought to force the authorities in free states to return fugitives from enslavement to their enslavers.

By the 1840s, several hundred enslaved people were escaping to free territories successfully each year, which made slavery an unstable institution in the border states. In the early 1800s, many free states petitioned to disregard the 1773 Fugitive Slave Act. The people of these Northern states did not consider it their responsibility to capture, jail, and return runaways to slave owners. Many jurisdictions pushed back on the Fugitive Slave Laws by passing Personal Liberty Laws. Under these local acts, it was mandated that before an enslaved person could be returned, they would be entitled to a jury trial. Others refused to hold a runaway in their jail or to assist in any way with the capture or return of a fugitive. These acts also allowed Northern states to nullify or invalidate any federal law they deemed unconstitutional. As a further blow to Southern enslavers, the Supreme Court of the United States ruled, in *Prigg v. Pennsylvania* (1842), that states did not have to offer aid in the hunting or recapture of enslaved people, significantly weakening the law of 1793.

To strengthen the 1793 Fugitive Slave Act, the 31st United States Congress (1849-1851) passed the Fugitive Slave Act or Fugitive Slave Law on September 18, 1850, as part of the Compromise of 1850 between Southern interests in slavery and Northern Free-Soilers.

The Compromise of 1850 was a series of measures passed by the U.S. Congress to settle slavery issues and avert secession. The crisis arose in late 1849 when the territory of California asked to be admitted to the Union with a constitution prohibiting slavery. The problem was complicated by the unresolved question of slavery's extension into other areas ceded by Mexico in 1848. In an attempt to satisfy pro- and antislavery forces, Sen. Henry Clay offered a series of measures that admitted California as a free state, left the question of slavery in the new territories to be settled by the residents, provided for the enforced return of runaway slaves and the prohibition of the slave trade in the District of Columbia. Support from Daniel Webster and Stephen A. Douglas helped ensure the passage of the compromise. Moderates throughout the Union accepted the terms, which averted secession for another decade but sowed seeds of discord.

The Act was one of the most controversial elements of the 1850 compromise and heightened Northern fears of a slave power conspiracy. It required that all escaped slaves, upon capture, be returned to the enslaver and that officials and citizens of free states had to cooperate. The Act contributed to the growing polarization of the country over the issue of slavery. It was one of the factors that led to the American Civil War.

Southern politicians often exaggerated the number of people escaping enslavement, blaming the escapes on Northern abolitionists, whom they saw as stirring up their allegedly happy slaves, interfering with "Southern property rights." According to the Columbus [Georgia] Enquirer of 1850, the support from Northerners for fugitive slaves caused more ill will between the North and the South than all the other causes put together.

The Fugitive Slave Act of 1850 compelled all citizens to assist in the capture of runaway slaves and denied enslaved people the right to a jury trial. Law enforcement officials were required to arrest people suspected of escaping enslavement on as little as a claimant's sworn testimony of ownership. It also placed control of individual cases in the hands of federal commissioners, who were paid more for returning a suspected enslaved person than for freeing them, leading many to argue the law was biased in favor of Southern slaveholders. The Act was broadly condemned in the North and prompted multiple instances of violent resistance.

Lynching and Vigilantism in the Pre-Civil War Years

In the late 18th and mid-19th centuries, lynching became increasingly associated with terrorism, murders, and punishment carried out with impunity, often in broad daylight and as a public event. Contrary to "frontier justice," an established criminal justice system was usually in place, but those carrying out the lynching bypassed this system. Lynching was driven by a strong desire for revenge, a lack of government criminal prosecution, and widespread public support. Initially, lynching did not necessarily mean killing, and vigilante "regulators" often punished crimes with tarring-and-feathering, beatings, and floggings. However, as vigilantism became more common, lynching evolved to become more synonymous with hangings and torture, including burning victims to death.

The first widely publicized incident of lethal lynching ("racial terror lynching" as it would come to be called) occurred in Madison County, Mississippi, in 1835, after a fabricated story of a planned slave uprising sparked local panic and resulted in the hangings of two White men and several enslaved Black people.

With the approach of the Civil War, the hostilities between abolitionist and anti-abolitionist factions escalated to a maddening frenzy. Between 1854 and 1859, vigilante groups from the Kansas and Missouri battled back and forth, resulting in the death of up to 200 people and property damage in the millions of dollars. This time of upheaval came to be known as Bleeding Kansas.

In the agrarian South, between 1790 and 1860, annual cotton production skyrocketed from four thousand bales to four million per year. Cotton became America's most important export commodity. During the same period, the demand for an expanded labor force to harvest cotton increased the slave population from seven hundred thousand to around four million. The increase in the production of cotton and the need for manual labor to harvest it put mounting pressure on the situation, ultimately contributing to the outbreak of the Civil War.

The Years of War and Reconstruction (1861-1877)

The number of lynchings began to escalate in the 1830s and became much more widespread during the era of Reconstruction in the American South following the Civil War. The emancipation of nearly four million enslaved people during the war brought a rise in White supremacy and racial terrorism. The targeting of ethnic minorities reached a crescendo in the U.S. between the 1890s and 1920s, primarily in the Southern states, because that was where most African Americans resided. Still, such targeting was not restricted to that region of the country or even to the African-American community. History records the lynching of many ethnic groups in cities in the North including Blacks, Whites, and Native Americans, and the lynching of Mexicans in the Southwest.

The Montana Territory holds the record for some of the deadliest non-Black vigilante actions during the Civil War years. From 1863 to 1865, hundreds of suspected horse thieves were rounded up and murdered in massive mob actions. Additionally, as had happened in California during the Gold Rush of the 1840s, thousands of gold-hungry prospectors descended on the Montana Territory in May 1863, after gold was discovered there. Most of these prospectors sought to enrich themselves through honest work, but others turned to robbery and theft as road agents, preying upon those who had rightfully obtained the gold. In the fall and winter of 1863-1864, these rogues were responsible for numerous robberies and the deaths of over 100 people. A vigilance committee near the gold fields was organized in December 1863, and in the first six weeks of 1864, at least 20 of these road agents were captured and hanged by the organization.

The gold supply substantially declined in 1865. Many of the fortune seekers who had not struck it rich in the fields attempted their hand at ranching. Cattle rustling and horse thievery were prevalent. As Montana had not yet obtained statehood, territorial law prevailed—several vigilante groups organized as a counter-action to the lawlessness. Between 1865 and 1870, the vigilantes had captured and summarily executed over an additional two dozen criminals.

In Texas, rumors of a slave insurrection resulted in the lynching of 30 to 50 Black slaves and 20 Whites between the years 1862 and 1864. In October 1862, in an incident now known as "The Great Hanging in Gainesville," 41 Unionists were hung over 13 days.

In the same year in Minnesota, a Sioux Indian uprising resulted in the murder of over 500 Whites after the natives became upset at broken government promises, corrupt Indian agents, and undelivered food and supplies. As a result of the uprising, 303 Native Americans were arrested and sentenced to die after a military trial. President Abraham Lincoln intervened and pardoned all but 38 of those convicted. Outraged, a mob of several hundred citizens attempted to lynch all 303 Santee Sioux. Determined actions by U.S. troops stopped the lynch mob. On December 16, 1862, the 38 unpardoned Indians were sent to the gallows, in one of the largest mass hangings in American history.

On July 11, 1863, massive anti-draft riots broke out in New York City and lasted for several days. Earlier that year, the U.S. government had instituted a mandatory draft to provide fresh troops for the Union. Anger among the city's sizeable Irish-born population, anti-government and anti-Black, escalated. As The Civil War Military Draft Act was written, one could escape the draft by posting a $300 levy. Poor Whites and other disenfranchised men were forced into the military, while the more affluent were able to avoid being drafted. Anti-Black violence was fueled by a well-established resentment that, because of emancipation, these Irishmen had been competing for some time against freed Blacks for jobs.

On the 13th, volunteer firefighters, angry at their commissioner, set fire to their company firehouse and proceeded to lead a mob of rioters down the streets of Manhattan, ransacking and burning businesses in their wake. Over that week, the riot continued; it was estimated that the crowd may have numbered as many as 50,000. They attacked businesses known to employ Blacks as well as the homes of prominent White abolitionists. The upheaval was put to rest on July 16th when President Lincoln rushed 4,000 troops into the city, some of which had just fought at Gettysburg.

The death toll for the six days of unrest was over 1,200, of which a large number were reported to have been African Americans.

In Southern states, at the end of the Civil War, emancipation finally came to the enslaved people after two and a half centuries of bondage. Four million formally enslaved persons were finally granted the status of freed persons.

Reconstruction-era lynchings, as well as thousands of largely unprosecuted acts of assault and terrorism during the period, would mark the most violent and deadly era in Black American history. During the 12-year-period following the end of the Civil War an estimated 2,000 Black people were lynched as Whites refused to accept the reversal of roles thrust upon them with the end of the war and the passage of the 13th Amendment.

Passed in 1865, the 13th Amendment to the Constitution abolished slavery in the United States. The 14th Amendment (1866) naturalized all persons born in this country, and the 15th Amendment (1869) gave them the right to vote while protecting formerly enslaved Blacks from racial violence.

In 1865, Congress established the Freedmen's Bureau, formally known as the Bureau of Refugees, Freedmen, and Abandoned Lands. Intended as a temporary agency to last the duration of the war, the bureau was placed under the authority of President Johnson's War Department one year after the war ended; most of its original employees were Civil War soldiers. Its goal was to help achieve economic, educational, and civil prosperity. The Bureau did some excellent work. It fed millions of people, provided medical aid, and built hospitals; it helped legalize slave marriages, find lost relatives, and negotiate settlements in some legal disputes. Many universities still in existence today—among them Howard University, Hampton University, and Fisk University—were established by the Freedmen's Bureau.

Unfortunately, few of the Bureau's lofty goals were realized. Instead, in the aftermath of the Civil War, much of the country had evolved into a time of oppression and racial terrorism. From the beginning, the Bureau faced resistance from various sources, including many White Southerners. The Bureau was set up to help the newly freed slaves and some poor Whites, who were promised they would be able to settle on land confiscated or abandoned during the war. However, after long deliberation, Congress voted that no ex-Confederate land would be given over for re-settlement.

Despite the Confederacy's defeat on the battlefield, the Southern citizenry resisted accepting that defeat, clinging to honor, manhood, and racial supremacy over "Negro Rule." This resistance led to mob violence and lynchings directed against Northern carpetbaggers, Southern Scallywags, and especially former slaves. In the years immediately after the War, thousands of Black people were murdered when they attempted to claim their rights.

This era marked the birth of the Ku Klux Klan and other hate organizations. Within three years of the KKK's birth in 1865, a Klan klavern could be found in every Southern state. With the founding of these groups, extralegal lynching grew to epidemic proportions. It was estimated that nearly 2,000 racial terror lynchings of Black men, women, and children took place in the American South during the Reconstruction era, 1865-1877.

The newly gained rights for former slaves provided by the passage of the 13th, 14th, and 15th Amendments would be short-lived; in early 1877, the outcome of the presidential election of 1876 was still in contention; allies of the Republican Party candidate Rutherford Hayes met in secret with moderate southern Democrats to negotiate acceptance of Hayes' election. The Democrats agreed not to block Hayes' ascendancy to the office of U.S. President on the condition that Republicans withdraw all federal troops from the South. This agreement, the Compromise of 1877, restored the Democrats to power in all the states of the old Confederacy. It also set the stage for a return to "home rule" in the region and would give rise to the era of Jim Crow, legalizing racial segregation. These statutes would marginalize African Americans and reverse the gains made by those amendments.

Nationwide resistance to racial equality resulted in the re-establishment of racial subordination through bias laws, disenfranchisement, and terrorism, most dramatically enforced through lynching.

Racial terror lynching of Black people defined a shameful era in America. These lynchings differed from the hanging of White people in places where there was no functioning criminal justice system. Racial terror lynchings, as well as thousands of largely unprosecuted acts of assault and terrorism, were directed at all Black people. They enforced compliance with racial hierarchy and White supremacy and ensured racial segregation and denial of equal rights.

Many lower-class Whites who did not own slaves or benefit from slavery before the war opposed the idea of a social revolution that would make Blacks their political and social equals. Even before the Civil War, non-slaveholding Whites defended slavery by serving as slave patrollers or joining posses and mobs because they feared rebellion and emancipation as much as did the plantation owners.

After the Civil War, these poor Whites turned to racism and lynching because they saw freed Blacks as competition for land and jobs, and it bonded them together as part of a ruling class.

Lynching 1877 to 1955

Between 1882 and 1968, Black people were the primary victims of lynching: 3,446, or about 72 percent of the people lynched, were Black. But they weren't the only victims of lynching. Some White people were lynched for helping Black people or for being anti-lynching.

In 1892, journalist Ida B. Wells was shocked when three friends in Memphis, Tennessee, were lynched. Black proprietor Thomas Moss operated a successful grocery business with two co-workers, William Stewart and Calvin McDowell. While their business flourished, one of their neighborhood competitors' businesses, owned by White grocer William Barrett, did not.

Barrett lodged a bogus complaint with the police against Moss, accusing him of waging war against his White competitor. For two days, racial tensions escalated. On March 5th, a sheriff and five deputized citizens, all White men, approached the rear of Moss's store; in self-defense, the three Blacks fired on the attacking mob, wounding three of the posse. The three Blacks were taken into custody and transferred to a local jail. Early on the morning of March 9th, the fourth day of the prisoners' incarceration, a mob of about 75 men overran and dragged the men out of the jail. The three men were dispatched to a passing steam locomotive at the rear of the detention center and taken to a railroad yard one mile outside of Memphis. All three were shot in the backs of their heads. McDowell was butchered to the point of unrecognition. The crime: the Black victims were lynched for the social crime of being the economic competitors of Whites.

Before the lynching of Moss, Stewart, and McDowell, Ida Wells had been content to be a local newspaper journalist. Outraged by the murders, she began a global anti-lynching campaign that raised awareness of the atrocities of lynching. This campaign became her lifelong mission through editorial writing, lecturing, and organizing anti-lynching societies.

In 1910 Ida Wells-Barnett (she had married Ferdinand Barnett in 1895) founded and became the first president of the Negro Fellowship League, which provided social services and community resources for Black men arriving in Chicago from the South during the Great Migration. She was also instrumental in founding the National Association for the Advancement of Colored People (NAACP).

Her in-depth investigation of lynchings dispelled the false narrative that attempted to justify lynching as a response to assaults of Black men on White women. She found lynchings were more an effort to suppress Blacks who competed economically with Whites, especially if they were successful. She encouraged Black women to participate in the anti-lynching crusade by organizing clubs such as the National Association of Colored Women. The organization aided African Americans by addressing civil rights issues such as women's suffrage, lynching, and Jim Crow laws.

By the 1890s, lynching had become markedly sadistic, especially when Blacks were the prime target. Extralegal vigilantism had moved light years from blacklisting, harassing, whipping, and tar and feathering; it had even eclipsed the simple act of hanging. With regularity, burning, torture, and dismemberment were used to exaggerate the humiliation and increase the suffering of the victim. Additionally, lynching in many cases no longer involved a spontaneous act of a mob turning violent, capturing a suspect, and committing a terroristic act. Instead, the person to be murdered would be held long enough for the local newspaper to print a special edition proclaiming there would be an execution. The period of delay was usually overnight, but in at least one case, a lynching was advertised two weeks in advance.

Public lynchings evolved into well-planned carnival events. In many cases, they were portrayed as family gatherings, as celebrations. Tens of thousands of people would come, bring their children, and prepare a picnic lunch so they could participate in the spectacle. During these pre-planned lynchings, food vendors and souvenir hawkers would flood the area and vie for the prime locations in front of the crowds to sell their wares.

In most cases, photos of these lynchings were captured by members of the mob who came to the scene with their personal cameras; but often, professional photographers would strike a deal with local officials to obtain prime locations from which they might photograph the gruesome event as it unfolded. These photographers captured the grotesque images of hung, mutilated, and burned Black Americans. Even more disturbing were the images of the celebrating spectators who, in many cases, posed with the remains of the victim. These photos were similar to the kind of photos that might have been made after a successful hunting trip where the hunters would pose with their prey, but at the lynchings, spectators would pose with the body of the man or woman who had just been murdered.

Photographers turned selling their photographs printed as postcards into a cottage industry. The penny postcards were saved as souvenirs, traded, and preserved as mementos of being part of the event. These cards were often mailed to loved ones with inscriptions such as "This Is the Barbecue That We Had Last Night," "This Is What He Got," or "Token Of A Great Day" written on the reverse.

In 1873, Congress passed the Comstock Act to forbid the publication of "obscene matter as well as its circulation in the mail." In 1908, the U.S. Postmaster General, backed by a Congressional amendment to the law, enforced the Act, adding lynching photographs and postcards to the list of banned obscene material. His actions did seem to curtail the mailing of these photographs and postcards, but in fact only drove the photographic commerce to disguise itself as innocent regular mail. Afterward, these cards were concealed inside an envelope or a mailing wrapper instead of being mailed open-faced as they had been before.

As if the possession of lynching photographs as mementos was not macabre enough, the ultimate souvenir to take away from a lynching would be a body part of the victim or at least a piece of the lynching rope used to hang him or her. In all too many cases, a lynching victim was tormented premortem. Fingers, toes, ears, noses, and lips were a common target by souvenir hunters. Castration was a punishment often perpetrated against the victim. This was especially true when the perceived charge against him had been sexual assault or some other offense against a White female. In one documented case, a group of teens collected the burned skull of a man. The boys knocked all the teeth from the cremated skull and then sold them as souvenirs for ten cents apiece.

The cases of lynchings decreased in American in the early 20th century. While the emergence of the Second Ku Klux Klan in the late 1910s intensified the number of extrajudicial killings, they declined with the stringent enforcement of the death penalty for those convicted of lynching starting in the 1920s.

The NAACP was credited with a significant win in 1915 with the Supreme Court's *Guinn v. United States* decision. This decision outlawed the "grandfather clauses" in certain state constitutions that allowed White men to vote without passing a literacy test as long as their grandparents had voted before 1867. It also gave registrars the discretion they needed to exclude Black Southerners whose grandparents had not been legally able to vote before the end of the Civil War. The *Guinn* decision encouraged African Americans across the South to undertake new initiatives to become registered voters.

A significant event in the late 19th century led to rumors of a potential war between the United States and Italy. This event was the largest single mass lynching in the U.S., which took place in 1891 in New Orleans, Louisiana, in which 11 Italian Americans and Italian immigrants were killed. In March 1891, 19 men, mostly of Italian ethnicity, were indicted for the murder of New Orleans police chief David Hennessy. Nine of the indicted men were tried for the murder, and of those, six were convicted, while a mistrial was declared for the other three.

The day after the trial, a large crowd, including some of the city's most prominent citizens, gathered outside the jail. This mob, which included a future Louisiana governor and a future New Orleans mayor, believed that organized crime had influenced the jury. On March 14th, the mob broke into the jail, dragged 11 of the Italian prisoners to the street, and then shot and mutilated them. Public sentiment at the time supported the mob's actions, as they were seen as stopping the influence of the Mafia. Consequently, Italy severed diplomatic relations with the U.S., and the U.S. implemented restrictions on Italian immigration for some time. This tragic event also contributed to the strengthening of the Mafia.

On the international stage, the U.S. was negatively perceived because of lynching and vigilante violence. Incidents such as the New Orleans lynching and the hundreds of other acts of violence around the country, combined with international pressure, moved President Benjamin Harrison to send the first anti-lynching legislation to the U.S. Congress. The attempt met strong opposition from Southern senators and the legislation never got out of committee.

As the 20th century began in America, there had been little anti-lynching legislation taken up by Congress. Neither of the two major political parties aligned with those attempting to stop the extralegal activities, and Jim Crow laws curtailed any gains that Blacks had made at the ballot box. It would be up to the African-American community to combat racial terror from the grassroots. Blacks singled out the Whites responsible for their oppression by refusing to frequent their businesses, refusing to seek employment from them, and, in some cases, burning their establishments.

Editorials written by the Black press helped spur these acts of defiance. Journalists like Ida B. Wells-Barnett and T. Thomas Fortune were instrumental in bringing to the forefront the atrocities of lynching. Using their voices through Black publications, these writers were able to encourage public education and actively protest and lobby against lynch mob violence.

The NAACP and related groups publicized injustices, investigated incidents of ferocity, organized demonstrations, and worked toward the passage of federal anti-lynching legislation.

Beginning in 1915, America saw a significant population shift known as the Great Migration. This event played a crucial role in reducing lynching and other forms of violence.

The oppression of Southern Black sharecroppers by unscrupulous landowners, racial discrimination, lynching, and unequal access to education prompted many to seek opportunities outside the South. Despite being freed through emancipation and given some chance for equality through organizations such as the Freedmen's Bureau, African Americans in the 20th century still lived in the grip of the Southern plantation economy. Only a few managed to break free from the pre-Civil War system of masters and slaves by purchasing land, starting their own businesses, or succeeding in other ways.

Without their own land to work, 3.9 million formerly enslaved individuals struggled to control their destinies after the Civil War; most continued as sharecroppers, farm laborers, or tenant farmers—a system only marginally better than slavery.

In a four-year period ending in 1918, coinciding with the end of World War I, 450,000 Blacks moved from the farms and fields of the South to Northern cities such as Chicago, Detroit, Pittsburgh, and New York City. Then by 1920, the floodgates truly opened, and almost 800,000 more had moved North. This migration from the South to the North and West would continue up to the early 1970s when the movement reversed, and Blacks began moving back to the South, escaping the urban conflicts, murders, and perilous living conditions in the large cities away from their homeland.

During WWI, losing five million men to the Armed Forces and limiting foreign immigration created a labor shortage in Northern and Midwestern cities. These employment openings in the North and the lack of opportunities in the South made a perfect combination of circumstances to spark the Great Migration of African Americans. However, just moving to the North did not solve all the problems that needed to be solved, and racial tensions increased in their new home cities, leading to riots and unrest. The rapid incursion of Blacks unhinged the racial balance in these Northern cities and aggravated the hostility between established residents and the newcomers. In the summer of 1917, racial riots broke out in East St. Louis, Illinois, Washington D.C., and Houston, Texas, as a result of labor tensions.

Under the impression that they might better their standings as citizens of America, when the U.S. entered into World War I, more than 350,000 African Americans volunteered to join the Allied war effort. Of this number, over 50,000 would see combat while serving with American Expeditionary Forces on the Western Front. Although this provided new opportunities for many African

Americans, resentment of these soldiers would go on to encourage widespread segregation and discrimination after the war ended and these servicemen returned home.

The end of World War I and the return of Black and White soldiers, combined with job market competition and an economic slump, all combined to lead to intensified unrest, rioting, and lynchings throughout the U.S.

Black men who had served with distinction during the war not only failed to receive respect for their military service but in at least 20 cases, Black veterans were murdered in the years 1919-1920. The majority of these incidents resulted from minor offenses, such as the alleged failure to give proper respect to White women. In one case, a Black man named Wilbur Little was beaten to death by a mob for not removing the Army uniform in which he had served. These attacks on returning Black veterans were fueled by the demobilization of tens of thousands of troops, Black and White, with little or no concrete plans for integrating them into the job market. Unemployment ran rampant, fueled by the number of returning troops, the removal of price controls, and the resulting inflation. By April 1919, 40 percent of 4.7 million men who had served America during the war were unemployed.

President Wilson recognized that the economy in 1919 was not capable of providing immediate employment for all the returning soldiers. Before the war, the nation was in a recession, but entering the war led to significant U.S. federal spending, causing a shift in national production from civilian to war goods. Unemployment decreased from 7.9 percent before the war to 1.4 percent, due partly to the creation of new manufacturing jobs and the removal of many young men from the civilian labor force through the military draft. However, with the returning soldiers coming home, the situation was expected to change.

The Red Scare

In July 1918, W.E.B. Du Bois, one of the founders of the National Association for the Advancement of Colored People, wrote an editorial in *The Crisis* (the official newspaper of the NAACP) in which he urged his fellow African-American countrymen to set aside their differences over the nation's treatment of its Black citizens and "close ranks" in the war against the Imperial Central Powers.

But ten months later, in May 1919, after witnessing the horrific treatment of Black soldiers returning from Europe to the United States, including the lynchings of several while still wearing the uniform of the U.S. Army, Du Bois wrote a very different editorial urging Black men and women to resist their treatment. That editorial read:

> We are returning from war! *The Crisis* and tens of thousands of black men were drafted into a great struggle. For bleeding France and what she means and has meant and will mean to us and humanity, and against the threat of German race arrogance, we fought gladly and to the last drop of blood; for America and her highest ideals, we fought in far-off hope; for the dominant southern oligarchy entrenched in Washington, we fought in bitter resignation. For the America that represents and gloats in lynching, disfranchisement, caste, brutality, and devilish insult—for this, in the hateful upturning and mixing of things, we were forced by vindictive fate to fight also.
>
> But today, we return! We return from the slavery of uniforms that the world's madness demanded we don to the freedom of civil garb. We stand again to look America squarely in the face and call a spade a spade. We sing: This country of ours, despite all its better souls have done and dreamed, is yet a shameful land.
>
> It lynches.
>
> And lynching is barbarism of a degree of contemptible nastiness unparalleled in human history. Yet for fifty years, we have lynched two

Negroes a week, and we have kept this up right through the war.

It disfranchises its citizens.

Disfranchisement is the deliberate theft and robbery of the only protection of poor against rich and black against white. The land that disfranchises its citizens and calls itself a democracy lies and knows it lies.

It encourages ignorance.

It has never really tried to educate the Negro. A dominant minority does not want Negroes educated. It wants servants, dogs, whores, and monkeys. And when this land allows a reactionary group by its stolen political power to force as many black folks into these categories as it possibly can, it cries in contemptible hypocrisy: "They threaten us with degeneracy; they cannot be educated."

It steals from us.

It organizes industry to cheat us. It cheats us out of our land; it cheats us out of our labor. It confiscates our savings. It reduces our wages. It raises our rent. It steals our profit. It taxes us without representation. It keeps us consistently and universally poor and then feeds us on charity and derides our poverty.

It insults us.

It has organized a nationwide and, latterly, worldwide propaganda of deliberate and continuous insult and defamation of black blood wherever found. It decrees that it shall not be possible in travel nor residence, work nor play, education nor instruction for a black man to exist without tacit or open acknowledgment of his inferiority to the dirtiest white dog. It looks upon any attempt to question or even discuss this dogma as arrogance, unwarranted assumption, and treason.

This is the country to which we Soldiers of Democracy return. This is the fatherland for which we fought! But it is our fatherland. It was right for us to fight. The faults of our country are our faults. Under similar circumstances, we would fight again. But by the God of Heaven, we are cowards and jackasses if, now that that war is over; we do not marshal every ounce of our brain and brawn to fight a sterner, longer, more unbending battle against the forces of hell in our own land.

We return.

We return from fighting.

We return fighting.

Make way for Democracy! We saved it in France, and by the Great Jehovah, we will save it in the United States of America—or we will know the reason why.

After reading the comments of Du Bois, President Woodrow Wilson, a segregationist, was enraged. In a private conversation, he expounded the belief that the returning Negro servicemen would be the greatest threat in conveying Bolshevism to the U.S.

The First Red Scare of 1919-1920 originated from the ultra-nationalism of World War I and the Russian October Revolution of 1917. Authorities considered the threat from labor unions as an attempt by far-left groups to spread socialism, anarchism, and communism throughout America. These same authorities also feared the threat posed by returning Black soldiers, who were now demanding racial equality and the right for targets of mob violence to defend themselves. These soldiers had faced the hostility of an oppressive Germany and its allies and had helped to defeat it. Upon their return, they were bent on confronting and defeating the hostility they had experienced in their own country.

President Woodrow Wilson did not want to leave these men to chance. In his State of the Union address, he urged Congress to welcome the soldiers with a job. Wilson urged Congress to focus not on those highly skilled or connected men who could easily find work but on the others who would find it challenging to obtain employment.

American factories produced 21,000 airplane engines, over 300 million pounds of explosives, 3.5 million rifles, and 20 million artillery rounds during the war. But with the war now over, there was a surplus of workers and a deficit of production plans.

Secretary of Interior Franklin Lane asked, "What shall be done with the Returning Soldiers? The ordinary and normal processes of the private initiative will only provide immediate employment for some of the men of our returning veterans. It seems to me important, therefore, that the development of public works of every sort should be resumed so that opportunities should be created for unskilled labor … that plans should be made for such developments of our unused lands and our natural resources …"

In 1919, debate over the Secretary's plan, commonly known as "Homes for Soldiers," was debated in hearings in the House of Representatives. Committees discussed the cost of homestead agreements for 640,000 soldiers, which was about $125 million in the first year. Unfortunately, by 1920, the United States was in a severe recession, and the plight of the returning soldiers worsened. Veterans found it challenging to work and complained of distant and unhelpful counselors. For Black veterans, the transition to civilian life was even worse. Military service had strengthened their claims to the full rights of citizenship, yet many returning Black veterans still suffered indignities and were harassed by White racists. Lynching doubled between 1917 and 1919, and cities across the country experienced horrible race riots that resulted in much damage and death.

The events in America became tumultuous in 1919. April to September that year, which came to be known as the Red Summer, was a period of nationwide terrorism and racial riots. The term Red Summer was coined by NAACP leader and author James W. Johnson; it was marked by hundreds of deaths and massive casualties across the U.S. Over 40 violent incidents in more than three dozen cities across the United States were reported.

The Omaha Courthouse Lynching of 1919

The Omaha Courthouse Lynching illustrates the upheaval during the Red Summer of 1919. This lynching was witnessed by an estimated 20,000 people, making it one of the most enormous individual spectacles of racial violence in the nation's history.

Charred corpse of Will Brown, Omaha, September 28, 1919 (Image Public Domain)

Omaha, Nebraska, a major center for meatpacking, had been a racial tinder box for several years. The major meatpacking plants hired Blacks as strikebreakers in 1917, and Omaha's working-class Whites had shown great hostility toward the Black strikebreakers. One of the packinghouse workers, a 40-year-old African American named Will Brown, was accused of raping a 19-year-old White woman, Agnes Lobeck. A local newspaper, *The Omaha Bee*, sensationalized the story by carrying details of the story along with photos of both Lobeck and her accused attacker.

After his arrest on Sunday, September 28th, Brown was taken to the Douglas County Courthouse. Soon, a mob of around 250 men and women marched from South Omaha and gathered outside the courthouse. When Omaha's Mayor Edward P. Smith arrived on the scene, he was attacked, and a rope was strung around his neck. He lost consciousness after being strung up to a lamppost. He was cut down before he succumbed to the attack, but the mob breached the courthouse doors and killed Brown. His body was then taken to the street, where it was hung from a lamppost and riddled with gunshots. His body was then tied behind a police car and dragged to an intersection in the middle of the city, doused with kerosene, and set aflame. Soon after the incident, photographs of the charred body and many of the lynchers were distributed around the world. The photograph became the iconic image of the violence of that Red Summer.

The Summer of 1919 also saw the devastating Elaine Race Massacre in Elaine, Arkansas, which occurred on September 30th, two days after the Omaha riot. A group of Black sharecroppers, the Progressive Farmers and Household Union, gathered in a church near Elaine to demand fair payment for their cotton crops from the landowners. Concerned about Communist influences, the landowners sent armed guards to disrupt the meeting, leading to gunfire and the death of two guards. Subsequently, mobs of White men from as far away as Tennessee descended on the area, indiscriminately killing Blacks. Although there was no official death toll, it was believed that five Whites and up to 250 Blacks were killed. Federal troops were called to round up Black citizens, and over 100 were charged with insurrection. Due to the widespread attacks on Black citizens, this incident can only be classified as wholesale lynching.

African-American resistance to lynching carried substantial risks. In 1921, in Tulsa, Oklahoma, a group of 75 African-American citizens attempted to stop a lynch mob from taking 19-year-old assault suspect Dick Rowland out of jail. In a scuffle between a White man and an armed African-American World War I veteran, a White man was shot, leading to a shootout between the two groups.

Whites retaliated by rioting, during which they burned 1,256 homes and as many as 200 businesses in the segregated Greenwood district, destroying what had been a thriving area. A 2001 state commission confirmed 39 deaths, 26 Black and 13 White. The commission gave several estimates ranging from 75 to 300 total dead. Rowland was saved, however, and was later acquitted.

Between 1930 and 1940, an additional 400,000 African Americans left the South, with another 3.3 million following suit between 1940 and 1960. This significant demographic shift reflected the continued migration of the Black population, which began with the Great Migration. Notably, the focus of this migration later shifted to cities on the West Coast, leading to substantial growth in Los Angeles; the San Francisco/Oakland area of California; Portland, Oregon; and Seattle, Washington.

1935 would be the last year that lynchings in the United States would reach double digits. Between 1936 and 1945, the number of lynchings dropped dramatically. The executive director of the NAACP attributed the decline to a shift in public discourse, anti-lynching activism, and the Great Migration. [7]

World War II, 1941-1945

African Americans have been fighting for this country since the French and Indian War in the mid-1700s. It is no surprise that over three million Black men registered for service in the armed forces following the introduction the Selective Service Act of 1940, and 1.2 million Black men and women served in uniform during World

---

[7] Lynching in America-Confronting the Legacy of Racial Terror, Equal Justice Initiative. P.55

War II, with half of them serving in both the European and Pacific theaters. Over four thousand of the 1.2 million who enlisted were Black women.

During World War II, African-American soldiers were eager to fight, but they faced discrimination due to Jim Crow rules in every branch of the armed forces. Many Black individuals were denied enlistment, even after the December 7, 1941 attack on Pearl Harbor that precipitated the United States' entry into the war. Those African Americans who were accepted into the military still experienced the segregation that led to separate facilities for African-American soldiers both within the United States and on the war front.

African Americans, often deemed unfit for combat service, were usually assigned to support roles, such laborers. They were commonly assigned as cooks, mechanics, road construction workers, stevedores, and truck drivers. Additionally, there were few opportunities for them to advance in rank, and those who did advance were allowed only to supervise other Black troops.

When Black units were allowed to excel, their military service became legendary. In the war's later years, the need for additional manpower compelled the military to begin utilizing Blacks as combat soldiers, in tank units, and as pilots.

In the fall of 1944, General George Patton's Third Army was driving at breakneck speed across France; Patton's order to the Third was simple, "Seek out the enemy, trap him, and destroy him."

On October 2nd, the 761st Tank Battalion, "The Black Panthers," joined Patton's Third Army. Addressing the men of this new unit, the General said,

> "Men, you're the first Negro tankers to ever fight in the American

Army. I would never have asked for you if you weren't good. I have nothing but the best in my Army. I don't care what color you are as long as you go up there and kill those Kraut sonsofbitches. Everyone has their eyes on you and is expecting great things from you. Most of all, your race is looking forward to your success. Don't let them down, and damn you, don't let me down! They say it is patriotic to die for your country. Well, let's see how many patriots we can make out of those German sonsofbitches."

The 761st first saw action on November 7, 1944, and was not relieved from service for the next 183 days. In December, the battalion aided the 101st Airborne Division when it was surrounded near Bastogne during the Battle of the Bulge.

After the Battle of the Bulge, the 761st cleared the way for the U.S. 4th Armored Division into Germany, breaching the Siegfried Line. They swiftly advanced through numerous German cities and towns. As the war in Europe neared its end, the 761st was one of the first American units to reach Steyr, Austria, and met with the 1st Ukrainian Front of the Soviet Red Army at the Enns River. By the time they reached the Enns, these men had helped liberate 30 towns under Nazi control. On May 4, 1945, the 761st, along with the 71st Infantry Division, liberated the Gunskirchen concentration camp; the German guards had fled shortly before.

The unit distinguished itself by earning a Presidential Unit Citation. In addition, members of the unit distinguished themselves, including Sgt. Ruben Rivers, who won the Medal of Honor. In addition, 11 Silver Stars, 56 Bronze Stars, and 246 Purple Hearts were awarded to members of the unit.

After the D-Day storming of the Normandy Beaches in June 1944, and until port facilities were established in Antwerp, Belgium, the Allies used over 6,000 trucks and 23,000 Army personnel to transport an average of 12,500 tons per day of supplies, ammunition, rations, gasoline, and weapons to the front for 83 days. This massive operation was named the Red Ball Express—after a U.S. railway tradition whereby railmen marked priority cars with a red dot. Black drivers predominantly staffed this enormous undertaking, many of whom had never driven a truck.

General Patton concluded these trucks to have been the most valuable weapons, and Colonel John D. Eisenhower, the Supreme Commander's son, stated that without the Red Ball truck drivers, "the advance across France could never have been made."

While the 761st Tank Battalion's commanders and the Red Ball Express's drivers were mechanized on land, in the skies above the Black Tuskegee Airmen protected bombing runs over Berlin.

The Tuskegee Institute, located near Tuskegee, Alabama, which educated Black men in their pilot training, was established in exchange for Black support to reelect Franklin Roosevelt for his third term. After its establishment, the program faced opposition, from discrimination by the local Alabama community to the Army brass looking for any excuse to abandon the "experiment," as it was dubbed. The initial candidates experienced the implementation of Jim Crow restrictions on base and off.

Whereas flight school for White pilots lasted eight weeks, it was nearly two years of consistent training in Alabama before the Black pilots were given the same opportunity. When the Army was queried why it took two years to train the Black students, they responded that they needed to find enough recruits to have an entire fighter squadron. However, the more extended training period was mainly because the Army was reluctant to allow the pilots from Tuskegee to join the fight.

When the unit finally entered the war in April 1943 as the U.S.

Army Air Corps 99th Fighter Squadron in North Africa, it was assigned P-40 Warhawk aircraft to escort the bombers. Even with the P-40s—an obsolete plane even before WWII—the Tuskegee escorts had an astounding record of protecting their wards.

By July 1944, these men of color were gallantly piloting lightning-fast North American P-51 Mustangs. They totaled a bomber-shepherding record unmatched by any other fighter group. These airmen were not simply given this prestigious equipment; they had certainly earned all the respect and accolades the planes reflected. The crews of the B-17 and B-24 bombers always sat a bit easier after looking out their canopies to see the "Red Tails" of the Tuskegee planes flying above and below their formations. The Tuskegee Airmen flew 1,600 combat missions and would earn more than 150 Distinguished Flying Crosses for their actions during the war.

During this time, in England and later in France, Blacks did not find the same discrimination they had experienced in the U.S. Liaisons between Black troops and White women were a common practice in Great Britain and Europe late in the war. When photographs of Black servicemen dancing with White British women were published in an American magazine, it sent shock waves through many American citizens.

Senator Theodore Bilbo of Mississippi went so far as to pen a letter to General Eisenhower to discourage Black soldiers from fraternizing with White women in the war zones. Bilbo wrote that "negrophile" forces were advancing social equality in America, which he warned "inevitably leads to familiarity, miscegenation, mongrelization, and in many cases intermarriage between the races." In July 1945, Mississippi Senator James O. Eastland expressed similar anxiety in a floor speech in Congress, stating that in Europe "the Negro has crossed the color line" and "has gone with White girls." He warned, "There will be no social equality … when the soldier returns."

At the war's end, the Black World War II veterans, just as had their fathers and grandfathers who had worn the uniform of the U.S. military before them, expected a hero's welcome and the respect due them for their service. Whereas the number of lynchings had not risen during the war (in 1946, there were only six lynchings reported in the U.S., and four of those deaths occurred during one incident), the level of racism certainly had. It began even before the returning troops disembarked from the transport ships. As soon as the troops had walked down the gangplanks, the segregation started anew. A sign greeting them on the dock stated that the White troops were to turn to the left and Blacks to the right to a marshaling area. The White forces later paraded down the streets of cities across the U.S. to the marching beat of a military band; the returning Black troops received no such welcome. Instead, there were numerous examples of violence against Black veterans.

Within a year, at least a dozen Black veterans were killed or attacked, some while still wearing their military uniforms, in part because the White communities they often returned to were threatened by Black veterans. Whites recognized that these veterans would come back and be leaders in the civil rights movement. In that context, the military uniform and the service of Black veterans were viewed as extremely dangerous, and it led to highly hostile treatment for a lot of veterans upon their return.

After the war, Black veterans were primarily excluded from the benefits created by the G.I. Bill of 1944. There was a wide disparity in how benefits were distributed, contributing to an even more significant gap between the races regarding wealth, civil rights, and education.

The G.I. Bill guaranteed low-interest mortgages and other loans; those loans were not administered through the Veterans' Administration but instead by local banks. White-run financial institutions refused to grant loans to Black veterans. Veterans of color who enrolled in vocational programs often were unable to participate in skills training because, in many cases, tools and equipment were available only to White students. Blacks were refused housing in Whites-only neighborhoods. Monies that flowed to many of these newly formed suburban neighborhoods were not available to the poorer city neighborhoods in which Blacks were relegated. Only about 100 of 67,000 G.I. home mortgages were issued to Blacks in New York City and the northern New Jersey suburbs. When it came to education, many did not attempt to take advantage of the bill's benefits because they could not afford to spend time in school instead of working. Black students of the 1930s had not been adequately prepared in the primary and secondary grades to compete on a collegiate level, and colleges in the North and South set admission standards unattainable for many Blacks. The VA itself encouraged Black veterans to pursue vocational training instead of seeking higher education, thus denying educational benefits to many students.

When the G.I Bill ended in 1956, about eight million World War II veterans had taken advantage of its benefits. Still, of that number, a substantial portion of Blacks had been left behind in receiving their share of education, housing, and wealth-building opportunities.

If Black veterans were no longer willing to accept second-class status, the establishment of voting rights became crucial. Across the nation, former soldiers led voter registration campaigns. White supremacists fought back, fearing that these registrations were the first step in racial integration and mongrelization; a wave of racist violence swept throughout the South. Widespread violence was almost an everyday occurrence during the 1946 electoral campaign. Blacks were warned to stay away from the polls, and in Georgia, the election of a White supremacist governor was celebrated by his supporters by attacks on those who had tried to cast a ballot against him.

Civil Rights Advancements in the 1950s and 1960s

The Civil War abolished slavery in 1865, but it was another 85 years before African Americans began to earnestly gain equal rights under the laws of the United States. In the mid-20th century, Blacks and other citizens mobilized and initiated an unprecedented fight for equality that spanned two decades.

In 1948, President Harry Truman issued an executive order to end discrimination in all military branches. This first step toward desegregation opened the door to a long struggle that would change the face of civil rights in America.

The advances made in the 1950s and 1960s emerged from the efforts of anti-lynching campaigns starting in the 1930s. Gains were made in the courts, allowing the NAACP to successfully challenge restrictive covenants in housing, discrimination in public facilities, and segregation in interstate transportation.

The first significant breakthrough of the 1950s occurred in 1954 when the Supreme Court ruled in *Brown v. Board of Education of Topeka* that racial segregation of children in public schools was unconstitutional. The Brown decision overturned the "separate but equal" ruling of the Supreme Court ruled in *Plessy v. Ferguson* (1896).

Less than a year later, on December 1, 1955, Rosa Parks was arrested when she refused to vacate her seat in a Whites-only section on a Montgomery, Alabama, bus. Her defiance set in motion a year-long boycott of that city's transit system and businesses, bringing Montgomery almost to its knees. The boycott was finally called off after the Supreme Court upheld the district court's ruling and struck down laws legalizing racial segregation on buses.

Not all gains were made by boycotts, sit-ins, and demonstrations.

A catalyst at the time was the ghastly murder of Emmett Till, a 14-year-old Chicago resident who, on August 28, 1955, was visiting relatives in Money, Mississippi. After working in the cotton fields in Money all day, Emmett and some other boys stopped at a drug store. Accounts of what transpired thereafter vary. Emmett, being from the North, was not accustomed to the Jim Crow laws of the South. Emmett started a conversation with the store's cashier, Carolyn Bryant, a White woman. It was reported that Till whistled at, touched the hand or waist of, or flirted with the woman as he left the store.

Two days after the incident, Carolyn's husband, Roy Bryant, and her brother-in-law, J.W. Milam, abducted the boy at gunpoint. They then severely beat him, gouged out one of his eyes, and killed him with a single gunshot to the head. They tied Till's body to a large metal fan and dumped him into a river. His corpse, barely recognizable, was discovered in the river on August 31st.

Emmett's body was returned to Chicago, where his mother, Mamie Till, held a funeral for her son. She refused a closed coffin, remarking that she wanted the world to see the brutality that had been visited on her son. Photographs of Emmett's mutilated remains were published in Black magazines and newspapers. The photos of Till's bloated and disfigured head and, later, a *Look* magazine article in which Bryant and Milam confessed to murdering the boy, became tipping points in the civil rights movement.

In the summer of 1957, nine Black students attempted to enter the all-white Little Rock (Arkansas) Central High School. This would be the first test of the *Brown v. Board of Education of Topeka* Supreme Court ruling. After discussions between the president of the United States, the governor of Arkansas, and the mayor of Little Rock broke down, President Eisenhower sent Federal troops to desegregate the school. Rather than bow to the forced integration by the Federal government, the Arkansas National Guard, sent by Arkansas Governor Orval Faubus, blocked the school's entrance. The following year, Governor Faubus closed all Little Rock schools. Little Rock Central did not reopen until 1960. This opposition to the integration of schools was not limited to Little Rock. As late as 1988 and as far away from the South as Boston, Massachusetts, racial tensions were still running at a fever pitch in opposition to the desegregation of schools.

President Dwight D. Eisenhower signed the Civil Rights Act of 1957 into law on September 9, 1957. This was the first substantial civil rights legislation since the Reconstruction period. The Act created no new rights but strengthened the voting rights set out in the 15th Amendment by establishing a Civil Rights Division within the Department of Justice and a Civil Rights Commission with the authority to investigate discriminatory conditions, and granting Federal prosecutors the power to obtain court injunctions against any interference with the right to vote.

Even though some civil rights activists were not convinced of the Act's efficacy, it was a stepping stone for more legislative action, such as the Civil Rights Act of 1960, which strengthened voter registration rights, and the Civil Rights Act of 1964, which banned discrimination by businesses, public places, and schools.

The 1960s became the decade of protest. It started in 1960 in Greensboro, North Carolina, with a sit-in by Black students at a Whites-only lunch counter, then continued with the Freedom Rides of 1961, the March on Washington in 1963, and the March 1965 from Selma to Montgomery, Alabama. The 1960s was also the decade of substantial legislative progress. This included the Civil Rights Acts of 1960 and 1964, the Voting Rights Act of 1965, and the Fair Housing Act of 1968.

Lynching had been perpetrated for a myriad of reasons: intimidation, White supremacy, terrorism, retribution for crimes such as sexual assault, horse theft, cattle rustling, or, as in the case of Wat Greer and David Neal in Shelbyville, for murder of a law enforcement officer.

In March 1981, in Mobile. Alabama, it would be the murder of a police officer that triggered a lynching with overwhelming ramifications in the annals of American jurisprudence. A mixed-race jury in Mobile acquitted a Black defendant in the murder of a policeman.

Henry Hays—the son of Bennie Hays, the second highest-ranking member of the Alabama KKK—and a man named James Knowles vowed revenge on a Black for the acquittal. While driving the streets of Mobile, they came upon Michael Donald, a 19-year-old man walking home. He had nothing to do with the murder of the policeman or the trial; he was simply walking home from a local gas station. Michael Donald was merely chosen at random for being black. Hays and Knowles called Donald to their automobile to ask for directions to a club in the area.

Hays forced Donald into the car at gunpoint and drove him away. After crossing into an adjoining county, the two forced Donald out of the car and into a wooded area near Mobile Bay. After exiting the vehicle, Donald attempted to escape but was caught and beaten with a tree limb. A rope was placed around the man's neck. Hays strung up the victim from a tree while Knowles continued to strike him with the tree limb. After Donald stopped moving, the two then slit his throat three times to ensure he was dead.

After the arrest of Hays, Knowles, and another man, the police investigation concluded that this murder was a drug purchase gone bad and released the three suspects. Beulah Mae Donald, the mother of the victim, insisted that her son had never taken drugs and that the police investigation was botched. She contacted Rev. Jesse Jackson, a national civil rights leader, who organized a protest march in Mobile.

The FBI investigated and was about to close the investigation when an assistant U.S. Attorney asked the Department of Justice to take yet another look at the evidence. Hays and Knowles were re-arrested and charged with murder and a civil rights violation. Henry Hays was found guilty by a jury and sentenced to life imprisonment, but the trial judge overruled the jury verdict and set the sentence at death. He was electrocuted by the state of Alabama in 1995. James Knowles was sentenced to life in prison. He was released in the 2000s. Henry Hays was the first White man to be executed for the death of a Black since 1913.

In 1984, Beulah Mae Donald filed a civil suit against the United Klans of America (UKA) for the death of her son. Three years later, an all-white jury ruled in favor of the plaintiff and awarded Mrs. Donald a $7,000,000 wrongful-death verdict and set a precedent for civil legal action against other racist hate groups. The verdict bankrupted the UKA.

Congress Passes Anti-Lynching Law, 2022

Although Presidents Benjamin Harrison, William McKinley, and Theodore Roosevelt tried to introduce anti-lynching bills during their administrations, it was not until 1918 that the U.S. Congress passed a bill. The Dyer Anti-Lynching Bill was introduced in the 65th United States Congress (1917-1919) by Representative Leonidas C. Dyer, a Republican from Saint Louis, Missouri, in the United States House of Representatives as H.R. 11279, in order "to protect citizens of the United States against lynching in default of protection by the States." It was intended to establish lynching as a federal felony and gave the U.S. government power to prosecute those accused of lynching. The bill called for incarceration, a $5,000 fine, or both, for city and state officials who failed to protect a person from being lynched; a $10,000 fine for the county in which a lynching occurs; and it permitted the prosecution of law enforcement officials who failed to protect citizens. The bill failed to pass in 1918 but was re-introduced in subsequent sessions. On January 26, 1922, it was passed by the House of Representatives; still, its passage was halted in the United States Senate by a filibuster by Southern Democrats.

Attempts to pass similar legislation were halted until the attempted passage of the Costigan-Wagner Bill of 1934. Subsequent bills followed, but Congress failed to make lynching a federal crime due to powerful opposition from Southern senators.

In 1901, George Henry White, the last former slave to serve in Congress and, at the time, the only Black member in Congress, proposed a bill to make lynching a federal crime; from that time to date, nearly 200 iterations of anti-lynching legislation have been introduced in Congress. Seven U.S. presidents, from Benjamin Harrison in 1890 to Harry S Truman in 1952, urged Congress to pass a federal anti-lynching law. In 2018, the Justice for Victims of Lynching Act was introduced in the Senate, aiming to recognize and apologize for historical governmental failures to prevent lynching. The Senate unanimously passed the act, but the House of Representatives took no action before the end of the session, effectively killing the bill.

Some 130 years after President Harrison attempted to move Congress to introduce civil rights legislation, they finally enacted an anti-lynching bill. On February 26, 2022, the Emmett Till Anti-Lynching Act, a revised version of the Justice for Victims of Lynching Act, was passed in the House of Representatives. A week later, the bill passed in the Senate and became law on March 29, 2022. An anti-lynching law, making lynching a federal hate crime, was finally enshrined in the American legal canon.

A single death is a tragedy; a million deaths is a statistic. These words were ascribed to Soviet leader Joseph Stalin, supposedly spoken in 1947.

One person being lynched is undoubtedly a tragedy; the lynching of thousands of persons in America since the 1700s should never be considered merely a statistic but, instead, an American travesty.

Acknowledgments and Credits

This volume would not have been possible without the gracious and substantial help of many individuals.

I am particularly grateful to Carol Roberts, Kathryn Hopkins, and Anna Frazier at the Bedford County Archives, who dedicated significant time to searching for and photocopying court records and other documents related to these murder cases.

Thank you to Trent Hanner and the staff at the Tennessee Library and Archives for assisting me in locating newspaper articles and maps of Shelbyville.

Thank you to Judy Phillips and Norm Williams for their contributions of photographs of the participants in these stories.

My heartfelt gratitude goes to Susan Havlish. She graciously accepted my request to edit this book, and her expertise in style, form, and editing significantly enhanced my writing.

Terry L. Coats
December 2024

References

Books

Berg, Manfred. *Popular Justice: A History of Lynching in America.* Rowman and Littlefield, 2012.

Brundage, W. Fitzhugh (Ed.). *Under Sentence of Death: Lynching in the South.* The University of North Carolina Press, 1997.

Equal Justice Initiative. *Lynching in America: Confronting the Legacy of Racial Terror.* Equal Justice Initiative. 2017.

Equal Justice Initiative. *Lynching in America: Targeting Black Veterans.* Equal Justice Initiative. 2017.

Kinchlow, Ben. *Black Yellowdogs: The Most Dangerous Citizen Is Not Armed, But Uninformed.* WND Books, 2008.

Legends of America. *Lynching, Hangings & Vigilante Groups.* Roundabout Publications. 2014

Newspapers

The Bristol Evening News, Bristol, Tennessee.

The Chattanooga Daily Times, Chattanooga, Tennessee.

The Chattanooga News, Chattanooga, Tennessee.

Knoxville Sentinel, Knoxville, Tennessee.

Lawrence Democrat, Lawrenceburg, Tennessee.

The Leaf-Chronicle, Clarksville, Tennessee.

The Nashville American, Nashville, Tennessee.

Nashville Banner, Nashville, Tennessee.

The Nashville Globe, Nashville, Tennessee.

Nashville Tennessean, Nashville, Tennessee.

The Shelbyville Gazette, Shelbyville, Tennessee.

Websites

Willard, Michelle (April 15, 2019). "Middle Tennessee Mysteries—Bedford County: Redin G. Purdy and Charles Henry." https://www.middletennesseemysteries.com/tags/2/bedford-county

Greene, Bryan (August 30, 2021). "After Victory in World War II, Black Veterans Continued the Fight for Freedom at Home," *Smithsonian Magazine.* https://www.smithsonianmag.com/history/summer-1946-saw-black-wwii-vets-fight-freedom-home-180978538/

Wikipedia. "Lynching." https://en.wikipedia.org/wiki/Lynching

Wikipedia. "First Red Scare." https://en.wikipedia.org/wiki/First_Red_Scare

Court and Legal Records

Circuit Court Records (April 3, 1912; August 14, 1912; December 10, 1912), Bedford County, Tennessee.

Register of Persons Committed to the County Jail of Bedford County (February 10, 1912), Bedford County, Tennessee.

www.ingramcontent.com/pod-product-compliance
Ingram Content Group UK Ltd.
Pitfield, Milton Keynes, MK11 3LW, UK
UKHW021025030225
454602UK00013B/859